PUFFIN BOOKS
Editor: Kaye Webb

THE BOER WAR

Often a fair-minded account of a war can be written only long after the fighting is over. Here is just such a history of the Boer War. It tells a story of courage, ignorance and mistaken beliefs – of the human strength and weakness shown by individual leaders on both sides. Many famous men were involved – Kitchener, Jan Smuts, Baden-Powell, Paul Kruger, Winston Churchill, Lord Roberts, Cecil Rhodes. Some won fame, others did harm to their own good repute. The Boers were amateur soldiers, and developed many ways of fighting that were then unusual in war. They became experts at guerrilla warfare – their small mobile forces attacked swiftly and then disappeared into a countryside they knew better than the enemy. The British fought back with a 'scorched earth' policy, and held many thousands of prisoners in their concentration camps – the 'invention' of Lord Kitchener.

The Boer War tells of a conflict where more people were killed by sickness than by bullets, and women and children suffered as much as the soldiers; it goes on to show how the compromises of the peace treaty helped to bring about the problems South Africa faces to this day.

James Barbary is the pen-name of a well-known author whose histories always make compulsive reading. This is a fascinating account of the Boer War and its effects.

D1392316

JAMES BARBARY

THE BOER WAR

PUFFIN BOOKS
in association with Victor Gollancz

Puffin Books: A Division of Penguin Books Ltd, Harmondsworth,
Middlesex, England
Penguin Books Australia Ltd, Ringwood, Victoria, Australia

—

First published by Victor Gollancz 1969
Published in Puffin Books 1975

—

Copyright © James Barbary, 1969

—

Made and printed in Great Britain
by Richard Clay (The Chaucer Press) Ltd
Bungay, Suffolk
Set in Monotype Baskerville

This book is sold subject to the condition
that it shall not, by way of trade or otherwise,
be lent, re-sold, hired out, or otherwise circulated
without the publisher's prior consent in any form of
binding or cover other than that in which it is
published and without a similar condition
including this condition being imposed
on the subsequent purchaser

Contents

Preface: How the Story Began   9

1. Trek!   13
2. The Racehorse and the Ox   26
3. *Mitzdruse to Schaffiger Bleimass*   35
4. Black Week   47
5. Escape to Freedom   63
6. B-P in Mafeking   75
7. A Case of Complete Surrender   87
8. Persevere to the End   105
9. Methods of Barbarism   118
10. Carry the War to the Enemy!   128
11. Peace at Last   142
    Further Reading   149
    Index   153

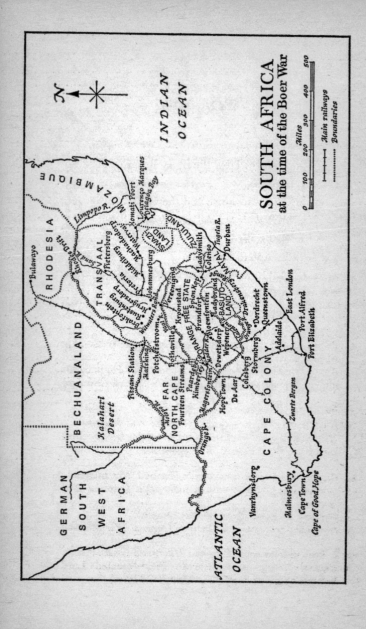

SOUTH AFRICA
at the time of the Boer War

Miles
0   100   200   300   400   500

++++++ Main railways
·········· Boundaries

INDIAN OCEAN

MOZAMBIQUE

Lourenço Marques
Delagoa Bay
Komati Poort

SWAZILAND

ZULULAND

Limpopo R.

RHODESIA

Bulawayo

TRANSVAAL

Pietersberg

Middelburg

Pretoria

Johannesburg

Krugersdorp

Brakfontein

Bronkhorstspruit

Potchefstroom

Mafeking

Magato

Tugela R.

Ladysmith

Colenso

Durban

ORANGE FREE STATE

Vereeniging

Kroonstad

Brandfort

BASUTOLAND

Bloemfontein

Bethulie

Drakensberg

Thaba Nchu

Wepener

BECHUANALAND

Pitsani Station

Vryburg

Kimberley

Modder R.

Fourteen Streams

Paardeberg

Magersfontein

Jagersfontein

Dewetsdorp

FAR
NORTH CAPE

Colesberg

Stormberg

Dordrecht

Queenstown

East London

Kalahari
Desert

Hope Town

De Aar

Orange R.

Adelaide

Port Alfred

Port Elizabeth

CAPE COLONY

GERMAN
SOUTH
WEST
AFRICA

Vanrhynsdorp

Zwarte Bergen

Malmesbury

Cape Town

Cape of Good Hope

ATLANTIC
OCEAN

Illustrations

1a Major-General Kitchener (*National Portrait Gallery*)
 b General Louis Botha (*Illustrated London News*)
 c General De Wet (*The Mansell Collection*)
 d Colonel Baden-Powell (*Illustrated London News*)

2a Cecil Rhodes (*National Portrait Gallery*)
 b President Kruger (*Kruger House Museum*)
 c President Steyn (*Illustrated London News*)
 d General Smuts (*National Portrait Gallery*)

3a An armoured train at the siege of Ladysmith (*The Mansell Collection*)
 b The Devons' charge on Wagon Hill at the siege of Ladysmith (*The Mansell Collection*)

4a British troops at Modder River in Black Week (*The Mansell Collection*)
 b A piper leads the Argyll and Sutherland Highlanders into an ambush at Magersfontein (*The Mansell Collection*)

5a British Mounted Yeomanry (*Imperial War Museum*)
 b A captured Boer Krupp gun (*Imperial War Museum*)
 c Colt machine-gun and galloping carriage. A Red Cross wagon on the left (*Imperial War Museum*)

6a British troops learn Boer tactics (*Imperial War Museum*)
 b Gordon Highlanders with a heliograph (*Imperial War Museum*)
 c Building a bridge (*Imperial War Museum*)
 d A military reconnaisance balloon (*Imperial War Museum*)

7a A Boer and his sons off to war (*Illustrated London News*)
 b General Cronje surrenders to Field-Marshal Lord Roberts at Paardeberg (*The Mansell Collection*)

8a British prisoners at Pretoria. Winston Churchill is on the right (*Radio Times Hulton Picture Library*)

  b Boer prisoners await transportation to a prisoner-of-war camp (*Imperial War Museum*)

  c Boer women and children flee Kitchener's 'scorched earth' (*Imperial War Museum*)

Maps

1   South Africa at the time of the Boer War   6

2   The Battle of Paardeberg   103

Preface: How the Story Began

By the year 1650, the merchant ships of little republican Holland, as well as trading busily along the American coast, had organized a commercial empire in the Spice Islands of the Orient. There was then no Suez Canal, so the Dutch had to travel to the Orient around the Cape of Good Hope in South Africa.

In a slow, old-fashioned sailing ship, the voyage out might take six months. The Cape had a pleasant climate, so the Dutch built a settlement there, for their ships to get supplies. They brought some tough Dutch farmers out from Holland. The Dutch word for 'farmer' was *landbouwer*, meaning 'tiller of the soil', which later was changed to *Boer*. The newcomers were given farms on easy terms, providing they sold all their produce, at fixed prices, to the Dutch East India Company, which owned the ships and controlled the settlement.

More Boers soon arrived, including West Germans, and French Protestants driven out of their own country by religious persecution. By the year 1700 there were thirteen hundred Boers in South Africa, and as their numbers grew, they began to make trouble for the Dutch authorities in Europe. They wanted to sell their produce on a free market at a good price, but the Dutch preferred to keep prices low, and profit from their monopoly. The Boers wanted above all to push the colony further inland, so that they could find new farms for their sons.

By 1800, the number of these tough and rebellious Boer frontiersmen had grown to 22,000. The power of the Dutch in the world was declining, and the British, now masters of India, had begun a worldwide struggle for dominance against the French under Napoleon.

9

When Napoleon's armies invaded Holland, the British sent soldiers to the Cape to protect their route to India. Once the Napoleonic Wars were over, the British paid Holland for the right to stay on in South Africa. The Boers, meantime, had evolved their own language, Afrikaans, and had become a distinct people, with their own church. They now found that these new governors, who spoke another language, also held ideas the Boers thought disagreeable. The British were opposed to slavery, for instance, and slowly began granting political rights to the Africans.

Three African races lived in South Africa before the Europeans thrust their way in. The Bushmen were the most primitive – cheerful little men, often with great artistic sense, and hunters and trackers so skilful they were capable of living off the desert, but at a Stone Age level of human cultural development. Since Bushmen did not make good farm servants, the Boers often hunted them down like wild animals.

The Hottentots had learned to breed cattle and live in villages. Good horsemen, they served as British soldiers, and responded well to the education given them by British missionaries. They gained the political rights of civilized men over a hundred years ago, and their descendants, now known as Cape Coloured, have only recently been deprived of them by today's Boers.

Much fighting went on against the Bantu, who were pressing on the British and Boer settlements from east and north. Over a stretch of sixty-five years the British fought nine frontier wars against Bantu warriors, and the fiercest, in Zululand and Matabeleland, had scarcely ended at the time the Boer War began. The Bantu, who still outnumber the Europeans several times over, were then cattle ranchers, but they grew Indian corn, too, and lived in settled villages. They had a religion based on ancestor worship, and held their tribal land in common. As ranchers themselves, the Bantu were the Boers' greatest rivals for land and cattle.

Until gold and diamonds were discovered in South Africa,

the British had no real interest in pushing the frontier much further inland, so the Boers, during the Great Trek, went ahead on their own, to create two new republics. The British had no effective means of stopping them, but they claimed a right to control the Boers, particularly when they oppressed the African peoples.

This long struggle for land and power lies behind the Great Trek, with which this book begins.

NOTE

At the turn of the century, a pound bought a great deal more than it does now. A sailor earned four shillings a day, and one pound a day was high wages.

Amounts of money mentioned in this book are expressed in English gold pounds of 1900.

I

Trek!

THE boy called Paul stood by the foremost pair of oxen, and looked back over his shoulder. There were sixteen red-and-white draft oxen in the team, glossy and beautifully matched. Paul was *voorlooper* – his job was to lead a way for the oxen to follow, and drag the big wagon behind them. They would move, at a plodding two or three miles an hour, through mountains and across rivers, into the unknown heart of Africa.

Would the other people back there, clustering around the wagon, never climb aboard and get going?

The women had to leave the house furniture behind, except for a few small tables and stools, and they had wailed about that. The men, pretending not to care, had taken one last, sad look at the *stoep* – the veranda – where so often they had smoked their pipes in the cool of the evening. A mountain of supplies was loaded into the wagon. Under that double canvas tilt – white on the outside, for coolness, thickly painted inside, to make it waterproof – every nook was crammed tight. There was a ton weight of supplies, including three hundred pounds of the most precious necessity of all, gunpowder.

And what if lightning struck us, thought Paul, shuffling his feet. That much gunpowder would blow the whole Kruger family to Kingdom Come.

For a boy of ten, this had already been an exciting year.

In the third year of terrible drought, locusts came over the hard clay of the waterless Great Karroo, where his father ran two thousand head of cattle across ten thousand acres. The locusts ate every leaf, every single blade of green, and the cattle sickened and died.

For a Christmas surprise, twelve thousand Bantu, armed with spears, had swarmed across the river from Kaffirland. They had burned four hundred and fifty homesteads, driven off stock, and left a hundred dead folk behind them, before the Boer commandos rode out to thrust the natives back across the river, and take Kaffir cattle to make up the losses.

Paul – trying to copy the steadiness of the lead oxen, who stood there stock still – reflected soberly that the grown-ups might be right: God had sent these afflictions to try the patience of His people. There was only one book in his house – a Bible. Paul thought of each daily happening in terms of stories from the Old Testament, which were read at family prayers every evening. The whole family of Krugers would sit around the table, and the Africans would squat quietly, with their backs to the wall, except for the little Bushman girl, given to Mother for a present, who had to be tied at night to the table leg, lest she run away.

The Chosen People, Paul told himself, as he waited for the crack of the whip and the single word of command, this very morning were leaving for the Promised Land.

Apart from all those other disasters that had made 1834 a bad year, something had come as a last straw – a final blow to their traditional way of life on the Great Karroo.

The British had been ruling down in Cape Town since they took over there from the Dutch at the time of Napoleon. Most of the up-country farmers, called Boers, were of Dutch or French Huguenot stock, and resented the British. When troops were needed to drive back invading Kaffirs, men like Paul's father would ride out happily on commando. That was proper work for a white man. Hunting antelope with a smoothbore flintlock was good, too. But no self-respecting Boer did any other work but hunt and fight, except to wait on his own stoep, at nightfall, and carefully count the heads of cattle when the African cattlemen brought them back from pasture. The Africans rode herd, and the white man had leisure to devote himself to the *lekker lewe*, the good life of hunting, making war, reading the Bible and bringing up his large family. The Boers thought it only right that the Chosen People – blue-eyed and fair-haired as Paul himself – should live off the fat of the land, as the Bible ordained.

Now the British down in Cape Town were going to change all that. An African could give evidence against his white master in a court of law – unheard of in times past! An African could now own land – in a country where there was scarcely enough land for every young Boer to find a farm of five or ten thousand acres, big enough to run his herd of cattle. The British had swept away the good old Pass Laws – which forced an African either to work for a master, or be arrested for vagrancy. And in the selfsame December when the Bantu crossed the river to burn Boer farms, the British had announced that from 1838 onwards – after a few years as apprentices – all slaves were to be free men, able to work for whom they pleased.

'The end of the world!' the old women muttered. Since the patience of the Chosen People – the Elect of God – was being tried beyond endurance, the men had acted. Paul was in on the secret, because his father, Hendrik Kruger, was wily Andries Potgieter's right-hand man. And Potgieter – six foot tall, slow of speech, with his cropped chin and clean-shaven upper lip, walking up to the wagon at this very moment in his short jacket and broken old straw hat – Andries Potgieter was a good man to follow in war and peace alike.

Potgieter went along the team now, making sure that the chain which yoked all but the wise old lead oxen to the *disselboom* was hooked fast. Paul Kruger felt Andries Potgieter's hand briefly touch his own shoulder. To be *voorlooper* – out in front to help the oxen over the hard places – was a serious job, and, at ten, Paul was the youngest to hold it. A Boer at sixteen was regarded as a man. Paul sighed; six more years to go.

In the cold weather last July, the men had sent out three

secret exploring parties. One went northwest, to Damara-land, but came back to say the land that way was too dry to grow feed or run stock. One party went north, across the Orange River and even further north, to the banks of the Vaal. The grass up there, they said, grew high enough to hide a standing man. There was water from springs and rivers. But though the days there, on the veld, were bright and sunny, the nights could be bitterly cold. Moreover, north of the Vaal River were the cattle lands of the dreaded Matabele, famous native warriors, an offshoot of the Zulus.

The third party came back from the northeast, from Natal, wearing broad smiles. Natal was a land dripping with milk and honey. Zulus to the northward, yes – but the fertile land to the south of Natal had lately been cleared of Africans in a native war. There was time to take and occupy the land before they drifted back. Rich soil, a pleasant climate, no frosts. Down on the shore, on a lagoon amid mangroves, lay Port Natal, where forty or so Europeans now lived. Supposing the Boers had access to the sea – a port of their own – they could then sell their hides, beef and tobacco to passing ships, and buy what stores they needed, with the British having no say in the matter.

Many people thought Natal sounded best, but wily old Potgieter had said, 'No, we go northward.' Paul's father had nodded consent on behalf of the Krugers, because he trusted Potgieter. When other people argued the merits of Natal, Potgieter explained. The British, who were too busy freeing slaves and fighting Kaffirs to want to take the interior of Africa for themselves just at present, might well let the Boers go northward, across the Orange River, into unclaimed land. But the British would never let people at all unfriendly to themselves occupy a seaport, which one day might be used as a hostile base to attack their ships on the way to India.

When they reminded Potgieter about those cold nights on the veld, and the savage Matabele, he smiled and shrugged. Potgieter was not good at argument, but Paul knew he would have thought out what to do.

At last, with a crack of Potgieter's hippopotamus-hide whip, as loud as a musket shot, came the long-awaited word of command:

'*Trek!*'

Paul pulled hard on the lead oxen, who rolled their big eyes, and snorted, and plodded the first step of the long journey.

Behind him, the women in the wagons began to sing a psalm.

From the rendezvous at Colesberg, just south of the Orange River, wagons were moving northwards in groups. Neighbours had to help each other over rough country. Up a steep pass a wagon might sometimes need two teams – thirty-two oxen – to keep it moving; or might even have to be taken to pieces, and fitted together again on the far side. The groups of neighbours travelling together could not be too large, either, because around each wagon rambled the family's flocks and herds. The flocks of too many trekkers moving together would eat off all the feed, and soon starve the stock.

Many of the African cattlemen had gone off to the British in Cape Town, to try the taste of freedom, so even boys as young as Paul were kept busy herding cattle. The best shots among the Boers rode out each day with their guns to kill antelope. Paul would see Africans come to the trail and smilingly offer to trade maize – in South Africa called mealies – or beans, or honey, for antelope meat. They had seen white men before – a few missionaries or traders – but never a whole people on the march.

During the ten years that the Great Trek continued, fourteen thousand Boers – people of mixed Dutch, French and West German descent, speaking a kind of old-fashioned Dutch called Afrikaans – decided to leave Cape Colony and head north. They were all members of the Dutch Reformed Church, all Calvinistic Protestants. They were not only crack shots but trained soldiers, because the British for years had used their commandos, or posses of armed horse-men, to guard the frontier with Kaffirland. They were trekking to find a land where each man could have a big farm for raising stock, and live at peace with a family of a dozen children, and a dozen or so black servants, hardly in sight of the smoke from his neighbour's fire.

Their smoothbore flintlocks were deadly up to a hundred yards – and a man who could unerringly hit the small knuckle of an ox with a flintlock at eighty paces was held to be a fair marksman. Crossing the Orange River, said the Boers, had washed away their British nationality; they, too, were free men now.

Most of the wagons diverged to the east, to the pleasant country of Natal, but a good few followed Potgieter and Kruger northwards, to the land of the Matabele. As the trekkers crossed the rivers, they named them. The Vet River was fat – swarmed with fat game. The Modder River was muddy. To right and left on the grassy plain, *kopjes* arose abruptly – flat-topped hills like buttes, their sides strewn with boulders. In the intensely clear air of the high veld, you could tell a river a long way off, by the row of light-green bushes – thorn and mimosa – that lined the banks.

Sometimes at night, when the wagons were outspanned, the men would hollow out an anthill for Mother to use as an oven, and bake bread. But usually it was meat, day after day. Paul looked sometimes at the withered fruit trees in the back of the wagon, carefully wrapped up in earth and sacking and wondered if they were still alive.

In May 1836, after they had travelled three hundred miles, Potgieter and his men outspanned by the Sand River, and held a council of war.

The Matabele had been in this fine cattle country for twenty years. Their main kraals were to the northwest, at Kapain, in the fertile Marico Valley. Their king, Mzilikazi, could put twenty thousand men into the field. A diet of milk and beef had made them all tall, broad-shouldered men.

Matabele warriors carried man-high, oval shields of oxhide. They wore a head-dress of black ostrich feathers, a band of otter skin across the forehead, and a loincloth made from the skin of the wildcat. Matabele fought Zulu fashion, in an *impi* of a thousand men each. They took the field in a curved formation, strong at the centre, outflanking at the wings, based on the horns of a fighting bull. Their weapons were a *knobkerrie* (a club of hardwood), a few throwing assegais, deadly up to fifty yards, and, most important of all, the stabbing assegai. When a Matabele 'dipped his blade in blood', he hissed. No other African tride had been able to withstand them in war.

Mzilikazi had already announced how he would treat white men travelling through the cattle lands of the Matabele. If they came 'one by one' – missionaries, or traders, or hunters – he would 'give them the road'. But those who came 'like armies' must take the consequences.

A family called Leibenberg crossed the Vaal River in their wagons, to spy out the land and seek feed for their stock. McDonald, a wandering Scot, who had served on the trek as schoolmaster, went with them. Word came that a wandering Matabele patrol had struck them down, killing eight, and four children as well. McDonald, who had taught Paul Kruger his catechism, was among the dead.

Potgieter at once called in all other wagons that had strayed beyond the Vaal. The council of war chose a place to give battle, a little hill between the Wilge and Rhenoster rivers. The hill was later called Vegkop – Afrikaans for 'battle'.

Fifty wagons were formed into a circle – or *laager* – and lashed together by trek chains. The women and children, Paul helping, went to cut thorn bushes, and stacked them in the gaps, and between the wheels. Four wagons, put together in the centre of the laager, were roofed over with planks and rawhide, as a shelter for the women and small children.

But some of the women, and boys, like Paul, who were large enough to ram powder down a musket, must stand by the marksmen, and load their weapons, if it came to an attack.

The horses were tethered inside the laager, but all the stock, including the precious draft oxen, had to be left outside. A laager made a good fortress, but Potgieter would have only forty or so marksmen, and Mzilikazi could send against him thousands upon thousands of warriors. Paul heard the men talk, and knew how it would be. The Matabele had no horses, and no guns. Their assegais would need to tear through four thicknesses of canvas, even to pierce the wagon tilts. Now, to throw those assegais, they would have to come within fifty yards. A flintlock musket in the hands of a Boer was deadly up to a hundred. Potgieter's marksmen would stand a chance.

While they waited, the men cast bullets, dropping molten lead into water, so it fizzed and hardened. The women nicked the big bullets with the sign of a cross, so each would spin open in flight, and inflict a ghastly wound. They poured buckshot into little greased skin bags for quick loading. At close range, one of those bags might knock over six Matabele at once.

In all, five impis came, and circled the laager out of range – five thousand Matabele, tossing their black ostrich-feather head-dresses, their spears black and spiky against the sky.

'I will go out,' said Potgieter soberly, 'and try speaking with them.'

One or two brave men mounted their horses, to follow him through a narrow gap between two wagons, which could be quickly closed.

As the tiny group of horsemen trotted forward towards the *induna*, or leader of the nearest impi, the Matabele announced their answer. Before peaceable words could be spoken, thousands of them moved as one man into formation, their feather head-dresses shaking. Spears and shield in hand, they made the fighting 'bull's head'. All hissed, as Matabele hiss when they strike with the spear.

Boer horses were trained to stand stock-still when hunting,

so the rider could fire from the saddle. Paul saw the horsemen rein in, well out of assegai range. There was a little volley – puffs of smoke, the bark of guns. The huge arc of armed Matabele moved, as if to swallow up the riders around Potgieter, who drew off faster, loading their muskets as they rode. Their horses again paused, rock-like. Again the riders fired – and now spurred, hell-for-leather, to the safety of the laager. The narrow entrance gap between the wagons was closed up, and stuffed with thorn.

Out of musket range, those five thousand Matabele sat down and waited. They knew that a long, silent wait was more exasperating than a quick attack would have been. The Matabele knew how to gnaw at their opponents' nerves.

To provoke them, Potgieter tied a red cloth to a whip-stock and waved it high over the wagons. The induna, as Potgieter had hoped, took it for a challenge. Five vast impis of warriors rose. Beating their oxhide shields like drums, they took up again the bullhead formation, and hissed as they moved forward.

'Hold your fire,' warned Potgieter.

The Matabele were within thirty yards before he gave the order to fire. The Boers fired again and again, as their women-folk and boys passed them hot-barrelled muskets, newly reloaded. Volleys of throwing assegais rose and fell in high trajectory over the tilts of the wagons. At point-blank range, the impis paused, as if baffled. They withdrew, leaving heaps of dying.

The Matabele attacked once more that day, and were again driven off. At long last they marched away, driving the Boer cattle and draft oxen before them. Two inside the laager had been killed by flying assegais, and every third man was wounded.

Potgieter and his friends were the pioneers, but others were coming up behind them. A group led by Gert Maritz had reached Blesberg; he sent up fresh draft oxen under armed guard. Paul Kruger's wagon was hauled back safely with the others, and there, at Blesberg, the trekkers adopted a Constitution. They elected seven men – the *Volksraad* – to make laws and judge those who broke them, and made Maritz president. They elected Potgieter commandant, and chairman of the council of war.

All this was young Paul Kruger's first taste of politics. As he heard the arguments, it dawned on him that his father and their friends were like the Jews when they entered the Promised Land, or like the Americans after the Revolutionary War. Here, on the high veld, they were bringing a new country into being, based on the power of an armed people.

First, Potgieter warned them, they must make this land safe from the Matabele. Two war parties went out that year. The first, a commando of 107 Boers, hit the Matabele kraals at Mosega at dawn, killed four hundred men, burned the huts, and brought back not only 7,000 cattle, but three American missionaries, who had crossed the Vaal to turn the Matabele into Christians.

One of them, the Reverend David Lindley, was a Southern Presbyterian. The Boers agreed pretty much with the Presbyterians, so they asked David Lindley to join them, since they had no ordained minister. Lindley helped them even further, by presenting the Boer leaders with a copy of the American Constitution, which enabled them to work out a satisfactory method of conducting elections.

Later that same year, 1836, 135 men rode off to attack Mzilikazi's capital, at Kapain. They fought from the saddle, skilfully keeping out of reach of the assegai but within gunshot range. In a nine days' running fight with the Matabele, they drove off another 7,000 head of cattle, themselves losing neither man nor horse. The Matabele went north, across the Limpopo River, into what is now Rhodesia, and lived there undisturbed for another fifty years. The Boers, having taken land and cattle from the black man, now settled down, to divide up the Transvaal into farms, and make it their own.

The news from Natal was also good.

Natal was separated from the settlements along the Vaal River – the high grasslands where the nights were cold – by a great mountain wall called the Drakensberg. Already, five good passes had been found through the Drakensberg. The neighbouring Boer settlements could keep in touch through the passes.

In Natal too, the trekkers had proved the superiority of fire arms and horses over the blind courage of Zulus armed with assegais. At the Battle of Blood River, they had fought and beaten Dingaan, the Zulu king. The anniversary, Dingaan's Day, is now South Africa's national day of rejoicing. Abandoning the land north of the Tugela River to the Zulus, the Boers, after a successful raid called the Cattle Commando, had driven southwards a huge herd of 36,000 Zulu cattle, and taken all the lands south of the river for their own. They had also kidnapped 1,000 Zulu children, and brought them back as 'apprentices', to herd the cattle for them.

Potgieter made his headquarters at Potchefstroom, north of the Vaal River. His men, too, went off raiding for 'apprentices' to labour on their farms. Soon, in the land where the Boers ruled, no African could take a drink or carry a gun. No African could go to the Dutch Reformed Church, or even, without his master's permission, ride a horse. The Boers were a handful, and they meant to keep in their own hands the means of power which had made the land theirs.

Suddenly, the news from Natal was not good any more, but bad. Potgieter had expected it all along.

The British would neither tolerate slavery so near their border, even though it might be called 'apprenticeship', nor were they willing to let Port Natal fall into unfriendly hands. Ports are rare on the African coast, and from Natal enemy warships might harass their traffic by sea.

In May 1842 250 British soldiers landed at Port Natal. Some were Inniskilling Dragoons, in scarlet. Others, a hateful sight to Boers, were Cape Mounted Rifles – all Hottentots, excellent horsemen and crack shots, riding ashore stiffly erect: black faces; green jackets; brown trousers. Behind, came two 6-pounder guns and a light howitzer.

Captain Smith, their commander, rode straight to the flag-pole in the port, where flew the *Vierkleur*, the flag of the new republic, and ran up the Union Jack. The Boers lay hidden in the mangrove swamp, shouldering their heavy elephant rifles, which could outrange a British army musket and could throw a four-ounce slug of lead-and-tin alloy, inflicting a terrible wound. They opened fire from ambush. In the first exchange of shots, the British lost forty-nine, killed and wounded. All the oxen hauling the guns were shot down, so the two 6-pounder guns fell at once into Boer hands.

The British dug in where they stood. Andries Pretorius, the Boer commander, knew of some Germans who understood how to serve and fire field guns. The bombardment of the hastily dug British trenches began.

Everyone supposed that the British could be starved out, but on one of the small islands out in the lagoon, called Bay Island, was a Scot named Cowie, loyal to the Union Jack. At night, he smuggled cattle across to the hungry soldiers. For the Boers to shift the British soldiers from those trenches meant facing their dreaded bayonets. It was stalemate.

Captain Smith, however, knew he had simply to hang on in those trenches long enough and the odds would change in his favour. Help came at last, in the irresistibly powerful form of the fifty-gun frigate *Southampton*. Past the headland into the lagoon sailed the frigate, towing behind her four whaleboats, each crammed with British soldiers, in the scarlet jackets of the 25th Regiment. Three hundred and fifty Boers ran to line the headland. They opened fire with their elephant guns, but a broadside from the frigate scattered them, and they ran.

Quietly, efficiently, the British took over Natal. They made a new treaty with the Zulus, confirming the Tugela and Buffalo rivers as the frontier. The British let the Boers who wanted to stay in Natal keep their farms. They confirmed their title to the land they had pioneered, and many who had gone on trek to escape the British decided, after all, to stay in Natal, since the country was so rich. But others would rather deny themselves the advantages of British peace, justice and security if it also meant rights for Africans. Under Jan Mocke these irreconcilables trekked, late in 1843, across the Drakensberg passes into the Transvaal, where Hendrik Kruger and his growing son, Paul, had found a home for themselves on a fine farm, called *Strydfontein*, or the Well of Strife. It was a significant name to start life on.

Later in the century, when the Boers again fought the British, Paul Kruger was to be their elected President. And none of this, that happened years before, would be forgotten.

2

The Racehorse and the Ox

A TALL, slender, fair-haired boy of sixteen stood on the deck of the three-masted sailing ship and looked with eager impatience at the bright green of the shore. He had reached Port Natal – now called Durban and a thriving port – after a sea voyage of seventy monotonous days. As the ship sailed along the coast of Natal, there had been tantalizing glimpses. Red sandhills rose up between wide sweeps of vivid green vegetation. He had caught sight of beehive-shaped roofs in Kaffir kraals.

The ship came into the island-dotted lagoon, where Boer had once fought British redcoat, and backed its sails. Sailors were lowering his leather trunk into a boat. At long last, he could stretch his legs in this enchanting new continent.

Not many men have had an entire country named for them. Cecil John Rhodes was looking for the first time, that morning of 1 October 1870, at the continent where, in years to come, his own name, amplified by two letters, would be printed large on the map: RHODESIA.

Cecil Rhodes's father was a clergyman in a small country town fifty miles north of London. Rhodes was one among eight brothers and two sisters, but at sixteen, when he had hoped to go to Oxford University, his health broke down. So here he was, on his way to join an elder brother called Herbert, who had a farm in the Umkomaas Valley in the colony of Natal. Herbert was trying to grow cotton, and had won his farm, yard by yard, from the bush.

Young Cecil Rhodes got his strength back working in the open air. An African farm, he soon found, was very different from farming in green, peaceful England. For one thing, white people in Natal were fewer than eighteen thousand, in a province inhabited by over a quarter of a million intelligent and warlike Bantu, who, during the past sixty years, had fought nine frontier wars against the British.

The farm the Rhodes brothers owned had once been Bantu grazing land. The hired labourers in their cotton fields were descended from Bantu warriors. This awareness that in South Africa the white man was hopelessly outnumbered, and therefore must impose himself, either by force or fraud, was for Cecil Rhodes an early lesson.

Cecil made friends with the son of a magistrate who lived a few miles away. Since both had lost their chance of a college education by coming to South Africa, the two of them, in the evenings, while tropical insects buzzed round the lamp, set themselves to study the Greek and Latin classics. Night after night, they lived imaginatively through the days when the ancient Romans built their empire by force of arms, bringing law and order to the barbarians who then inhabited France and Spain, until at last they managed to subdue even those wild, painted savages, the Britons themselves.

By Christmas, Cecil Rhodes was left single-handed in charge of the farm, with its mob of Bantu labourers to control. Herbert had heard of a better way of making money in South Africa than by uprooting thorn bushes and planting cotton. He left his brother to sell the farm for what it would fetch, and follow him up-country.

Three years before, a little girl, living near Hopetown, on the Orange River, had picked up a pretty stone, and taken it home. It was a diamond. The next year, more diamonds were found, in an arid stretch of no-man's-land called Griqualand West. When, in 1869, a single stone worth £25,000 was picked out of the blue diamond-bearing clay, there was a world-wide rush to the diamond diggings. Herbert Rhodes got there among the first.

From Natal to Griqualand West was a long and dangerous

trek – more than four hundred miles. Six months later, Cecil Rhodes had managed to sell the farm. He bought an ox wagon, and carrying with him a pick, two spades, several volumes of the classics, and a Greek dictionary, he set out alone for the lawless boomtown called Kimberley.

Rhodes trekked past Basutoland, the mountain homeland of armed and independent African horsemen whom the white man had never subdued. He made his way across the bare, dry veld, dotted with the lonely farms of the Boers, Paul Kruger's folk, who were hospitable to the English boy travelling alone, even though they might, at the same time, hate the British Government.

At Kimberley, forty thousand fortune hunters were living in tents or corrugated-iron shacks. Water was expensive, and every day thirty wagonloads of newcomers arrived. The town was thick with a fine white dust that filled the lungs and tormented the eyes.

The diggers wore high boots and corduroy trousers. They often went around shirtless, but every man had a leather belt with a long knife in it, and many carried firearms. Claims had been staked out across every inch of Colesberg Kopje, the hill where diamonds had been found in quantity. To Rhodes, at first sight, it looked 'like an immense ant heap, covered with black ants'.

Though these white men were called 'diggers', they did no actual digging. Rhodes soon found that, at Kimberley, the black men did all the pick-and-shovel work, while their white masters sat at tables, sorting out precious stones from the earth hauled out of the claim.

At the end of each day's work, the Africans were rigorously searched, to make sure they had found and hidden no diamonds for themselves. A small but extremely valuable diamond could be concealed in a bandaged cut, or swallowed. A boy of seventeen who wanted to make his fortune on the diamond fields had to keep his wits about him, and be pitiless.

Not long after Rhodes arrived, Colesberg Kopje had

entirely disappeared – much of it into the fine, white dust which infested Kimberley everywhere. Instead of a hill, there was now a hole, going deeper and deeper into the ground, a crater held up by scaffolding, crisscrossed with claims. The diamond-bearing earth was hauled up on winches and taken to where Cecil Rhodes sat, amid the others, on an upturned bucket, at a low table, wearing soiled white trousers, and hunting for precious stones in the midst of violence.

Already, after two years in Africa, he had prospered. He was building up his fortune with the quick wits of an ancient Greek, and the ruthlessness of a Roman. By the age of nineteen, thanks to a contract he won in partnership with an older man, C. D. Rudd, to pump out some flooded mines, Cecil Rhodes was within striking distance of becoming a rich man. But when most men would have pressed on to snatch their first million, Rhodes decided otherwise. He spent much of the year 1873 on a long journey into the interior of Africa. He then made an even stranger decision – to return to England, and study at Oxford University.

At Oxford he began the humdrum round of lectures and essays, but a chill, caught rowing in his college boat, got worse in the damp, raw English climate, and once more affected his chest. Rhodes, after only six months, was sent back to the dry, sunny uplands of South Africa.

He found the diamond diggings at Kimberley in a more chaotic mess than ever. With some of their wages, the native labourers were buying guns and smuggling them back to their kraals. They were getting drunk on Cape Smoke, a deadly, adulterated alcohol. Stolen diamonds were bought and sold every day; violence and bloodshed were commonplace. Most serious of all, too many stones were being dug up. Now, if diamonds should be thrown all at once, in quantity, on the world market, the price would tumble. Diamonds might no longer be considered precious.

But just suppose, Cecil Rhodes reflected, that all the diamond diggings in South Africa were controlled by one corporation. It would sell what stones it chose, at a fixed price, and quickly make an enormous fortune.

All this, at twenty, Rhodes proceeded systematically to bring about.

The tall, fair-haired man, with the face of a student, became a familiar figure among the diamond speculators. Men who underestimated Rhodes lived to regret it. He formed more partnerships; he bought out claims; he was ruthless with rivals, implacable to enemies, generous to his friends. In a remarkably short time, Rhodes and his partners controlled two thirds of all the diamonds in Kimberley.

A former *kopje walloper* called Barney Barnato controlled the rest. (A kopje walloper was a man who traded in stones that others had dug up.) Barney Barnato had arrived in South Africa from the East End of London with £30 and forty boxes of bad cigars. Now he was rich – and soon would be richer. As soon as Rhodes and Barnato had come to their understanding, a monopoly of diamond mining was established which every year grew stronger.

By twenty-three, Rhodes was chairman of the corporation which dominated the diamond business. He had already made a fortune such as most men only dream of, and political power, too, was within his grasp. That might have satisfied most ambitious men, but Rhodes was strangely unlike others. Off he went to Oxford again, and until 1881, when he received his B.A. degree, he attended to the world's diamond business only during college vacations.

Although making money was important to Cecil Rhodes, his ideas and dreams were more important still. His secret vision was that world peace might be secured by the domination of 'the Anglo-Saxon race'. ('Under the Stars-and-Stripes,' he once said, 'if it can be obtained in no other way.')

An important step, as he saw it, was British control in the heartland of Africa, all the way from Cairo to the Cape of Good Hope. And the Boers stood in the way.

Rhodes, though now a grown man, had something boyish

about him, still. When he spoke, words poured out of his broad, manly chest in a curious, high-pitched voice which, at times, rose to a shrill falsetto. The Bantu, who give nick-names to everyone, called him 'The Man Who Separates the Fighting Bulls'. This name showed their respect for his power, but also hinted that he might be mad, since only a madman tries to separate fighting bulls.

Rhodes wore a slouch hat, and tucked his more-or-less white trousers into high-buttoned boots. He showed no interest in women and never married, but he ate ferociously and was fond of drinking a mixture of stout and champagne called Black Velvet. Sometimes he would drink it all through the day, from breakfast until bedtime. Rhodes had a strangely hypnotic effect on other men, which could lead them to devoting their entire lives to fulfilling his prophetic ideas.

One man, however, among all others, loathed Cecil Rhodes. That man was Paul Kruger, who called him 'one of the most unscrupulous characters who have ever lived'. Of Rhodes, Kruger once said, 'No matter how base, no matter how contemptible, be it lying, bribery or treachery, all and every means are welcome to him if they lead to the attainment of his objects.' Others, however, saw in Rhodes an English gentleman, an Oxford graduate, immensely rich but less concerned with accumulating money than with spending it to make his country great and bring civilization to the backward peoples of Africa, including, perhaps, the Boers themselves.

Some admired Paul Kruger, seeing in him the patriotic leader of a small people struggling to be free. Others thought of him as an obstinate, unintelligent, narrow-minded man, living in a dim, heroic past and holding up progress.

Rhodes and Kruger first met face to face in 1885, when Rhodes, at thirty-two, was already a power in the land.

The land-hungry Boers were spilling over the edges of the Transvaal. They had set up two small republics, called Stellaland and Goshen, which straddled what Rhodes saw as the all-important British way north, up the old 'Missionaries' Road', through Bechuanaland. If tiny Goshen kept its independence, there could be no British railway, running from Cairo to the Cape, through the heart of Africa.

With five thousand troops at his back, Cecil Rhodes entered Goshen and for the first time met Paul Kruger. The British soldiers pitched camp at Fourteen Streams, and represented a silent argument that even Kruger could not ignore. Negotiations were not easy. Rhodes wanted to define the Transvaal boundary so as to leave a way clear for the British to go deeper into Africa. But, if anyone went deeper into Africa, Kruger could see no reason why it should not be the Boers.

Kruger, already a man of sixty, had won the last presidential election in the Transvaal on a policy of strictness in religious observance, and complete national independence. At fourteen, after completing the Great Trek, Kruger had killed his first lion. As Rhodes could plainly see, the thumb of his left hand was missing. A youngster alone out in the wilds, Kruger had amputated it himself, with a penknife; and, when gangrene set in, had fought the gangrene with turpentine. He was a man, not of books and business, but of long and tough pioneering experience. He and Rhodes were a total contrast.

Paul Kruger wore a black frock coat. The skin around his mouth was shaven, but the whiskers under his chin were thick. He had thick eyebrows, a coarse nose, and his hair, parted on the right side, was slicked down with grease. He looked like a cunning old backveld farmer, come to market with his crop, rather than the leader of a people. But he was not a man to underestimate.

He noticed that the British troops, commanded by Major-General Sir Charles Warren, were, for the first time in his experience, not wearing their traditional scarlet, but had been dressed in drab corduroy jackets and Bedford cord breeches, uniform that would not stand out, like a perfect target, on the sand of the desert or the dry grass of the veld.

Could this mean the British might secretly be preparing to fight a war, here in Africa?

To a confidant that night, after a day of hard negotiations, Kruger said of Rhodes, 'That young man will cause me trouble if he does not leave politics alone and turn to something else. Well, the racehorse is swifter than the ox, but the ox can draw greater loads. We shall see.'

Those five thousand British soldiers weighed heavily in the balance. The land of Goshen lost its independence. The Boers kept their title to the land they had pioneered, but the frontier was redrawn, so that the road to the north remained open for the British. Rhodes had won the first round.

Transvaal, or the South African Republic, as of late years Kruger had preferred to call it, was democratic to the point of bankruptcy. It had no army because, in case of trouble, the Boer farmers, all crack shots, would ride out voluntarily on commando. The state had a very small income. Boer farmers were as unenthusiastic as most people about paying taxes, but since they lived off the produce of their farms, they needed very little money, except to buy essentials like cloth, iron, coffee and ammunition. As late as 1885, the South African Republic, a sovereign state, could barely raise a foreign loan of £5,000, because no foreign banker trusted her ability to pay interest on such a vast sum.

Then, in 1886, something took place which increased the state revenue of the Transvaal from under £180,000 in 1886 to over £600,000 the following year, and to £1½ million by 1889. Paul Kruger's government of pious veld farmers suddenly became rich.

Two prospectors called Struben were wandering one day across the high ground between Pretoria and the Modder River when they found an outcrop of quartz which was showing through the dried grass. The quartz was gold-bearing and ran underground for an immensely long stretch, in a reef called the Witwatersrand. This one reef, the 'Rand', was in time to produce half the gold mined in the world.

South African gold is not alluvial – that is, it is not found in such easily worked material as sand, silt or gravel which can be handled by a single man employing shovel, pick and rocker. To get gold out of quartz, skilled miners are needed who know how to mine deep into hard rock, as well as expensive plants to crush the quartz, and chemical equipment to extract the gold. Only businessmen with large capital at their disposal could exploit the gold-bearing reef of the Rand.

Into these goldfields poured men of all nations – the *uitlanders*, as the Boers called them – for work at high wages. Natives came from their kraals to work in the mines, and to buy liquor and guns with their earnings. Another centre of vice and violence mushroomed up – the city of Johannesburg, where marble palaces and tin shacks stood side by side. For miles around Jo'burg stretched the farmers' republic of the Transvaal, sparsely populated by God-fearing Boers.

When someone came up to Petrus Joubert, the Transvaal's most experienced soldier, with the joyful news that gold had been discovered on the Witwatersrand, his answer was strangely prophetic:

'Instead of rejoicing, you would do better to weep, for this gold will cause our country to be soaked in blood.'

3

Mitzdruse to Schaffiger Bleimass

MITZDRUSE TO SCHAFFIGER BLEIMASS ABSOLUTELY
THAT CHAIRMAN HABLOHNER ON FLOTATION NO
REQUEST OR LETTER IN HOBELSPANE AS ANLEGSPAN IS
AUSGERODET AS PREVIOUSLY ANGELSTERN.

When a man like Alfred Beit, the financial wizard who was
Cecil Rhodes's lifelong business partner, sends a mysterious
telegram like this from a public post office, someone is likely
to puzzle out his meaning. There might be a fortune in it.

The secret which hid behind mysterious messages like
this, in a code which now means nothing to us, was discovered by Rhodes's enemies, and led him to disaster.

By the year 1895 the foreigners from all over the world who
had flooded to the gold diggings around Johannesburg outnumbered all the Boer farmers in the Transvaal by two to one.
The uitlanders paid five sixths of the taxes, but had no hand
in making the laws. They had no vote, no right of public
meeting out of doors, and, though they paid nine tenths of
the cost of the school system, their children were taught not
in English, but in the Dutch dialect called Afrikaans.

However, since the uitlanders were not in their own country, why should they complain of not having citizens' rights?

To this, the uitlanders had a simple and angry answer.
The British in Cape Colony were more tolerant. The tens of
thousands of Boers who had chosen to stay behind at the time
of the Great Trek enjoyed all the rights which the uitlanders
in the Transvaal were now demanding. In Cape Colony,
under British rule, four inhabitants out of five had the vote,

whatever their colour or language. The Boers, as well as voting, could use their own language in the courts and schools. In the Transvaal, by contrast, only one white man out of three had the vote, and the black man not only could not vote but was not even allowed to walk on the pavement.

Both Boers and uitlanders had good arguments. But what counted most was the fact that Cecil Rhodes, since 1890 Prime Minister of the Cape, supported the uitlanders. He saw that, by getting the vote for the uitlanders, it might be possible to take political power in the Transvaal away from men like Kruger. He dreamed of a federated South Africa, including the two Boer republics, the Orange Free State and the Transvaal. The Orange Free State, between the Orange and Transvaal rivers, had no uitlander problem, because it had no vast population of immigrant miners. But the threat of British encirclement gradually drove the Boers of the Orange Free State to join a common cause with the Transvaal government under Paul Kruger, which, thanks to the mines, was both richer and in a more dangerous plight.

And Rhodes was an immensely rich man, with influence on newspapers all over the world. Men in Europe and America, therefore, got to hear only the uitlanders' side of the story.

Of course, the uitlanders in the goldfields were not the angels that Rhodes's newspaper propaganda made them out to be. Jo'burg was a wild, wide-open city, and the men there were tough and rough and often crooked. But, undeniably, President Kruger bore down on them hard.

The Boer government had for years lived frugally on small taxes that were hard to collect. The sudden influx of millions in tax money from the goldfields broke down the stern Calvinist morality of some of the men around the President, though not of grim old Kruger himself. It was openly said that the quickest way to get results from the Transvaal government in Pretoria was by means of a bribe.

Even the big mining corporations, however, who could afford a bribe, had serious complaints. Mining at deep level in the hard gold-bearing quartz meant an extravagant use of dynamite, and Kruger had granted a dynamite monopoly to a man called Lippert, which cost the mining companies £600,000 a year. In this way, though, Kruger got what he wanted – lots of money to buy rifles, and a dynamite factory so constructed that it could be converted at a moment's notice into a factory for making ammunition. Since the days of the Great Trek, the Boers had got what they desired by fighting, and Kruger believed they might soon have to fight again, to keep what they had. If that time came, he would be ready.

One day a simple but fatal idea flashed into the mind of Cecil Rhodes. Since the foreign miners in the Transvaal out-numbered the Boer farmers by two to one, what was to stop them from taking over the country by force of arms? They might need a little help from the outside, which he would gladly pay for. London politicians, keen to 'solve the Boer problem' without need of an expensive war, might not be sorry for such a secretly organized uprising, of which they could take advantage if it succeeded, and pretend not to know about if it failed. (Though when had Cecil Rhodes ever failed?)

In public, Cecil Rhodes spoke of cooperation with the Boers, of equal rights for all white men south of the Zambesi. In secret he began to plot. Was it right for the Prime Minister of one country to encourage armed conspiracy against a neighbouring country in times of peace? Would Kruger's low opinion of Cecil Rhodes be proved true, after all?

Telegrams that began with words like *mitzdruse to schaffiger* began to be passed across the counters of South African post offices, and the plot thickened.

The conspiracy had three centres of activity – Jo'burg, among the foreign miners; a place called Pitsani, north of Mafeking in Bechuanaland, where armed horsemen could be secretly brought together to ride at a given signal to the uitlanders' aid; and finally Cape Town, where Rhodes, as

Prime Minister, could use his influence to entangle the British Government in London within his spider's web of intrigue.

In 1895 a new government was elected in London. For the next seven years, Britain would be run by Conservatives, pledged to strengthen the British Empire. Some men in the British Government undoubtedly had a shrewd idea what Rhodes had in mind, though publicly they were later to deny all knowledge. Others, no doubt sincerely, thought that the wider the bounds of the British Empire went, the further civilization was extended. Others, however, were more prudent. They wanted to have nothing to do with underhand conspiracies. Even if Rhodes succeeded, there would be many Conservatives in London who would condemn him for having chosen to gain his ends by violent and immoral means.

What secret motives might his important political friends in London have for supporting Cecil Rhodes? Consider the case of Lord Randolph Churchill, father of Winston Churchill, a former Conservative Chancellor of the Exchequer, who, since he died in 1895, cannot in any way be blamed for what came after. Lord Randolph, like many other British politicians, had been given a special opportunity to invest in Rhodes's gold-mining companies. In 1891 he bought stock costing £5,000. Four years later, when he died, this stock was already worth £100,000. Had he lived another year, it could have been sold for £250,000 – growing in value fifty times over in only five years. Rhodes, who often gave away mining stock in exchange for political favours, had, no doubt, with his golden touch made or increased the fortunes of many men in positions of power.

But even the politicians most friendly to Rhodes, though ready enough to take advantage of the conspiracy if it succeeded, would condemn him if it failed. And this he knew.

Rhodes relied chiefly on his greatest friend, a Scottish doctor called Leander Starr Jameson. A few years before, Dr Jameson had led settlers and armed police across the Limpopo River, to the land where the Matabele had fled. There he fought a private war, with Rhodes's money, to add another province to the British Empire – the country now called Rhodesia.

Dr Jameson – 'Doctor Jim', as people called him – was small, cheerful, extremely brave, and irrepressibly confident. The Doctor was now busy once more, recruiting 'policemen' and bringing them to his headquarters at Pitsani, a small, tented camp in the dry country of Bechuanaland, where inquisitive eyes were discouraged.

Doctor Jim's recruits were supposed to be protecting the new railway from Kimberley, the diamond city, to Bulawayo, in Rhodesia. The line passed through Mafeking, and there were soon enough 'policemen' encamped near by to make it the best-protected stretch of line anywhere in the world.

The Doctor had already recruited 510 men from the disbanded Imperial Police, and 110 from the Bechuana Border Police. Some of the young, adventure-loving British army officers sent out to serve in South Africa had already come under the spell of Rhodes's fascinating personality. Men like these, soldiers by profession but adventurers by temperament, began also to drift to Pitsani.

The ex-policemen from Bechuanaland were formed into two troops, under Captain the Honourable Charles Coventry. A hundred men in Mafeking, in the service of the Imperial government, under Major (Sir) Raleigh Grey, were warned in a whisper to stand by. The conspiracy had the air of a schoolboy lark – tremendous fun, real adventure. Hadn't Rhodes successfully pulled off similar wild enterprises in Goshen, not to mention across the Limpopo?

By November 1895 Jameson told Rhodes that, when the signal was given, he would have fifteen hundred armed men at his back at Pitsani, for a dash across the border into Transvaal.

Rhodes himself, in Cape Colony, had managed by pulling strings, to get as High Commissioner – the British Government's local representative – a man called Sir Hercules

Robinson, over seventy-one years of age, and a sufferer from insomnia. Sir Hercules was enthusiastic about Rhodes's dream of a solid British stripe down the map of Africa, stretching from Cairo to the Cape of Good Hope. He was a trusting old man, and easy to deceive.

The young officers and adventure-loving ex-policemen at Pitsani supposed that all would go well: surely the British Government had a shrewd idea what they were doing? With the honest and peace-loving men among the British officials at the Cape, Rhodes had a trickier job. He let these men believe that the uitlanders in the Transvaal were so oppressed that they were likely to make a perfectly spontaneous armed uprising of their own accord. If armed Britishers nearby rode to their aid, it would only be natural. Everyone concerned heard a different story. Only Rhodes himself knew the whole of it.

As fizzy and mind-confusing was this conspiracy as Black Velvet – Rhodes's favourite mixture of stout and champagne – which he was inclined to drink, a pint at a time, a little too early in the morning. His followers liked to drink it, too.

The miners of Jo'burg, in sober fact, were not at all sure they wanted to take part in an armed uprising. Some merely wanted the rights of a Transvaal citizen. Others would like to make the Transvaal British. Others dreaded the arrival of strict British justice. Really, only the handful of Rhodes's personal followers in Jo'burg could be fully depended on, at a signal, to come out on the streets, rifle in hand.

But would that matter? The important thing was that some sort of more-or-less convincing insurrection should take place. Newspapers all over the world would write it up as a proof that the uitlanders were oppressed, as Rhodes had always said they were. Dr Jameson's men would have been given their pretext to ride in – and their action would surely force the British Government to intervene.

Dr Jameson was already carrying around in his pocket a

letter, undated, but signed by Sir George Farrar, leader of the British community in Jo'burg, appealing to him to come and 'succour our women and children from armed Boers . . .' All that remained was to write in a suitable date – and, to newspapers all over the world, it would sound like an urgent cry for help.

Nothing Rhodes had done so far was a secret, however, to President Kruger. Too many clumsily coded telegrams had passed across post office counters. There had been too many loud whispers between tipsy or high-spirited Englishmen in public places.

'I will wait,' said Kruger, 'until the tortoise puts out his head.'

Rhodes had insisted from the start on one thing. If there should be no rising of the uitlanders, there must be no raid across the border.

If poor, persecuted uitlanders came out, gun in hand, to defend their women and children, who outside South Africa would be churlish enough to object should British policemen, who happened to be nearby, come riding to their aid? But if a party of armed men – a private army – were to invade a neighbouring country in time of peace, for no good reason at all, the best newspaper publicity in the world would not save the cause of the uitlanders from disgrace.

Rhodes, in Cape Town, and Jameson, at Pitsani, were in touch by telegraph. Beginning with Christmas Day, the wires began to hum. The uitlanders were expected to raise their revolt some time between 28 December 1895, and 4 January 1896.

At Christmastide, the Boers trekked in from their veld farms to celebrate the Christmas communion service of *Nachtmaal*. They carried arms, but that was not unusual. They all stayed on in town, waiting to celebrate the holiday of the New Year with the traditional fireworks and fusillade.

Cecil Rhodes, from Christmas Day onwards, went to stay in his splendid house at Groote Schuur, near Cape Town, with its magnificent library and private zoo. He was broodingly silent, men said, like a sphinx. He telegraphed Jameson three days running – on 27, 28 and 29 December – warning him to hold his hand. He knew Doctor Jim was optimistic and energetic, always ready to anticipate success.

No rising in the Transvaal – no armed men across the border. That must be clearly understood.

At midday on 29 December, a Sunday, Cecil Rhodes received a telegram which had been sent the night before. All knew, by now, that there had been no rising of uitlanders, and probably never would be. Yet, even so, Dr Jameson announced that with five hundred armed men behind him, he would cross the border and ride to Johannesburg.

Rhodes was flabbergasted. This was sheer folly. The telegraph office was closed for Sunday. Time was lost in getting it open. Rhodes wrote out a message, forbidding the raid, but the telegraph key was dead. Somewhere along its hundreds of miles of route, the wire connecting Mafeking with Cape Town mysteriously had been cut.

Rhodes went back home, to Groote Schuur. The game was up. He sent for Sir Graham Bower, secretary to Sir Hercules Robinson – an official deeper in the conspiracy than most. Bower found Rhodes sitting hopelessly on his bed, muttering, 'Jameson has ruined me and wrecked my life's work.'

What, in fact, had happened at Pitsani?

Part of the blame can be put on Dr Jameson's natural optimism and overflowing energy, and part on the effect of Black Velvet upon the professional efficiency of young officers.

So much work and money and planning had gone into the conspiracy, so much was at stake, that Dr Leander Starr Jameson could hardly bear to think he might be cheated of success. Had the Old Man – as Rhodes's followers called him – ever failed in anything he attempted?

Of course, these perplexing telegrams kept arriving from Cecil Rhodes – on the twenty-sixth and the twenty-seventh and the twenty-eighth – warning the Doctor not to move. But Dr Jameson felt sure he could read his friend's mind. The Old Man was Prime Minister, after all. In public he must discourage the raid – in private, of course, he wanted it. To Doctor Jim's lively mind, these telegrams obviously meant the opposite of what they said.

How big did that rising in Jo'burg have to be, anyway?

The handful of Rhodes's faithful followers there, at the very least, would appear on the streets, gun and flag in hand. The world might still be made to believe it was a real armed insurrection. Rhodes could then tell the newspapers what to print. Once everybody believed the uitlanders had risen 'to succour their women and children', the government in London would be compelled to step in and take over. Doctor Jim put a recent date on Sir George Farrar's convenient letter – *20 December*. The raid was on.

Cheers rang out into the night sky at Pitsani, and the necks were quickly knocked off champagne bottles, to toast success to the enterprise.

Out went a trooper, to cut the telegraph wires to Pretoria, so President Kruger in his capital should be kept from all news of what was happening. Intoxicated as he was on liquor and optimism, the trooper made a thorough job of it.

He began by cutting long strands from a farmer's barbed-wire fence – and burying them. At some point in this strange proceeding he must have felt that the telegraph poles hereabouts were uncommonly short. Barbed wire was not telegraph wire, either. When he saw a wire strung between high poles, he climbed up and cut it, most efficiently. But the wire he had cut was the telegraph from Pitsani to Cape Town, along which Rhodes's message might have come that Sunday, forbidding their fatal enterprise.

The wire to Pretoria, however, went on working, as usual, so President Kruger knew – as he had known all along – every move the raiders made.

President Kruger gave orders to Commandant Piet Cronje, who had fought against the British over twenty years before, when they tried to control the Transvaal by introducing garrisons of redcoats but had been badly defeated, and withdrawn. Cronje, small, barrel-shaped, heavily bearded, led his commandos out wearing a broad-brimmed hat and a frock coat, looking like a preacher riding circuit. His men were ready and waiting – when they came in for their Christmas communion, they had brought their guns. Off they rode, to confront Jameson and his five hundred hotheads.

The raiders under Doctor Jim had got as far as Krugersdorp, midway between Johannesburg and Pretoria, when the armed commandos of old Piet Cronje blocked their way. The bearded Boer farmers, armed with rifles, were mostly in their good go-to-church clothes. They confronted mercenary horsemen, most of whom wore articles of clothing from their police or army service.

There was a running fight across broken country, in which the British raiders took hard punishment. Six of Cronje's commando were killed. Next day, at Doornkop, Dr Jameson, finding himself surrounded, raised the white flag. There was nothing left to fight for.

Cronje promised to 'spare the lives of you and yours', but privately advised Kruger to deal with the raiders sternly. Some, in the Transvaal, wanted to hang Jameson's men from the same roof beam as had been used to hang the martyrs of the first Boer rising against British rule, in 1816, at Slagter's Nek. Boer memories were long and bitter.

Meanwhile, the handful of Johannesburg conspirators, taken by surprise, hardly had time to get out on the street and raise a flag before they had fallen into Kruger's net. The police had been waiting, and they used Dr Jameson as a hostage, warning Rhodes's followers in Jo'burg that, unless they too surrendered, Jameson and his raiders would die. In all, Kruger arrested sixty men – some genuine conspirators, others being merely those who had fought hardest for votes for the uitlanders. But who cared about the plight of the uitlanders now? Who would give votes to men who had plotted to overthrow an independent republican government by violence?

The fiasco rang around the world.

The Germans at once saw their opportunity. The Kaiser began to dream of a German protectorate over the Transvaal. He had one warship already in Delagoa Bay, and sent another down there from Zanzibar. He telegraphed his congratulations to President Kruger on having dealt with the raid, 'without appealing for the help of friendly powers'. But, though Kruger hated the British, he did not entirely trust the Germans, either.

The Kaiser wanted to land a force of German marines, and march them up-country, to 'guard' the German Consulate General in Pretoria. Once he had introduced armed men into the Transvaal, the Kaiser hoped he might, in the end, gain control there. President Kruger replied sarcastically that if the German Consul General was afraid, he could have fifty Boer soldiers for a guard. The Boers simply wanted their own country for themselves. But was that possible in the modern world of vast, jostling empires?

Rhodes at once resigned as Prime Minister of the Cape. Though he kept up a pretence of not knowing about the conspiracy, no one really believed him.

The raiders, Dr Jameson at their head, were finally handed over by President Kruger to British justice, and were given terms of imprisonment in Holloway Gaol – extremely short terms, considering the offence. The Colonial Secretary, Joseph Chamberlain, an orchid in his buttonhole, got up in the House of Commons to plead the innocence of Cecil Rhodes. He did it very well, but not everyone believed him. Kruger, when asked why he had dealt so mercifully with the raiders and uitlanders, said, 'It is not the dog who should be beaten, but the man who set him on to me.'

The Jameson Raid was in fact no schoolboy prank, but the longest step yet taken towards a terrible war.

During the following year, President Kruger increased the Transvaal's annual spending on arms from under £100,000 to nearly £500,000.

The British, also, began to take precautions and make plans.

4

Black Week

LONDON sent out a new High Commissioner. Sir Alfred Milner, in 1897, was forty-three years of age, a man of great intellect and energy. Milner had been an enormous success in Britain's most recent imperial possession, Egypt. He believed as passionately as Cecil Rhodes in the importance of the British Empire.

Milner described his post in South Africa as 'an awful job', but declared it was 'a fighting post . . . fighting all the time'. He had a complicated task. A large country going to war with a small one wants the rest of the world to think that right is on her side. Milner knew quite well that there were many influential people in Britain opposed to imperialism. He knew that the Boer republics had powerful foreign friends, like Germany, who must be discouraged from coming to her aid. War must always be prepared first diplomatically and psychologically, until the enemy is isolated and left without friends. Milner knew, therefore, that he must continue to speak of peace, while preparing the ground for the war that many imperialists now believed was inevitable. The rest of the world must see him trying to bargain when he was also getting ready to fight.

Sir Alfred Milner's public utterances, therefore, might sound reasonable and fair-minded; in fact, later he liked to describe himself as a Liberal. But oxlike, obstinate Paul Kruger was his enemy. He knew that nothing but force would shift Kruger, who never for one moment was deceived by his words. In 1898, for example, Milner declared mildly to President M. T. Steyn of the Orange Free State, 'We don't want the Transvaal, any more than the Orange

Free State, but only fair treatment for British industry and capital in the Transvaal, and an abstention from intrigues with foreign powers.' This seems a very reasonable remark, until one stops to ask exactly what 'fair treatment' means. In a negotiation, it could mean whatever a man like Milner wanted it to mean. Time would soon show that it meant nothing.

Kruger's dynamite monopoly was the issue that irked the gold-mining companies most, but Milner declared he had no mind to fight on 'a capitalists' question, pure and simple'. Milner was looking for an issue that would look well in the eyes of the world, and he found it, at last, in the franchise.

At one time it had been fairly easy for an uitlander, if he wanted, to become a Transvaal citizen, but a man now had to renounce his former citizenship, and wait fourteen years. Surely, if uitlanders lived and worked in the Transvaal, and paid taxes, they should at least have a chance of becoming citizens more easily? The outside world, Milner judged, could readily be made to think so. Rhodes still had great influence over the press, and all news from South Africa began, insensibly, to be contaminated with war propaganda. 'All political questions in South Africa,' warned Sir William Butler, a political figure with Liberal sympathies, 'and nearly all information being sent from Cape Town to England, are now being worked by . . . a colossal syndicate for the spread of systematic misrepresentation.' The psychological preparation for war had begun.

Paul Kruger knew as well as Milner what easy access to citizenship for the uitlanders would mean. 'It is my country you want,' said Kruger. 'It is our independence you are taking away.' And Milner, when negotiating over the franchise, did nothing to conciliate the touchy old President. At a reception given by President Steyn of the Orange Free State, for example, Milner pointedly refused to shake Kruger's hand. 'If we give them the franchise, we give up our republic,' said Kruger, 'since our burghers are outvoted by two to one.' However, to avert war, the old President offered to reduce the waiting time from fourteen years to nine, thus granting a 'nine-year franchise'.

Now came the critical part, in Milner's revealing phrase, of 'the great game between ourselves and the Transvaal, for the mastery in South Africa.'

Kruger was slow to give way, but at last, with great misgiving, he offered a seven-year franchise.

Joseph Chamberlain, Colonial Secretary in London, warned Milner that 'no one would dream of fighting over a two-year difference in franchise'. This revealing phrase implies that what Chamberlain and Milner sought was not so much agreement about the franchise as an excuse for going to war which would sound plausible to neutral nations.

Both sides had already begun to sense that this negotiation could come to no good end. The Boers had already spent much of their tax money on buying arms, mostly from Germany. They had field guns from Krupp, and modern Mauser rifles, deadly accurate in Boer hands up to a mile, or seventeen times the effective range of the flintlocks with which, years before, they had fought the Matabele. These rifles were superior even to the very latest Lee-Metford rifle, with which, in 1899, the British infantryman was to be armed. Kruger, now that his people were well equipped to fight, began, towards the end, to use the negotiations mainly to stave off war, at least until October, when the grass would have grown to feed the commandos' horses.

However, he made one last effort to test British sincerity.

On 19 August, President Kruger conceded the five-year franchise. This, of course, was the franchise the British had originally demanded. Joseph Chamberlain, in London, ordered Milner to refuse!

'It is perfectly clear to me,' said Jan Christian Smuts, Kruger's 28-year-old Attorney General, 'that Milner is planning to make war.' Yet Smuts himself, in secret negotiations, offered yet further concessions, in the desperate last-minute hope of averting an armed conflict. The Boers of the older generation might think they could beat the British, as they had done in small skirmishes years ago. They did not understand, as did the younger and better-educated men, like Smuts, that they would be taking on one of the greatest powers in the world.

Milner might feel cheerful about making war, but not everyone in London was ready to back him up. The British War Office certainly was unprepared. In January 1899, the British garrison in South Africa had amounted to only two cavalry regiments and six infantry battalions. In June, when the conference between Kruger and Milner failed, there was a call for reinforcements. Ten thousand men arrived at the end of August, giving the British a total, for the time being, of 27,000 troops, against the 60,000 men Presidents Kruger and Steyn could call on, to ride out on commando. The Boers, now that there seemed little chance of escaping war, might do well to act quickly.

In England, there remained an entire Army Corps of 47,000 men. Once the British ordered it to be mobilized and shipped to South Africa, Kruger knew for sure that war was inevitable. He dare wait no longer. On 9 October, he sent a forty-eight-hour ultimatum: Unless the British took their troops from his borders, and sent their reinforcements home, a state of war would exist.

Forty-eight hours later, the Boer riflemen, waiting eagerly along the passes of the Drakensberg, rose in their stirrups, raised their rifles, and, wildly cheering, rode down into Natal.

Did this small farming people, in fact, stand the slightest chance of defeating the greatest empire in the world?

Yes – if only they could reach the coast before the British Army Corps arrived.

Their rifles were better weapons than those of the British, and the Boers could shoot straighter. They had seventy pieces of modern artillery, and their *staats artillerie*, in drab uniforms with blue facings, many of them trained professionally by Germans, knew how to handle these guns effectively. Certain of their weapons, like the pom-pom – a Maxim automatic machine cannon firing one-pound shells very rapidly – were ideal for fighting on the open veld, and the British simply did not possess them.

The Boers would be fighting, moreover, across country they knew intimately, and moving their troops on 'interior lines'. They could switch their men rapidly from one front to another, while the British would have to transport them around the edge of South Africa, having begun by bringing them eight thousand miles across the ocean.

The commando system had its weaknesses. Discipline was lax. Men would get restless, and slip away home. In a crisis, a Boer army might begin to melt away. The fundamental Boer weakness, however, was the same as the fundamental British weakness. The Boer commanders were mostly old men, veterans of small-scale fighting against the British twenty years before. Generals like Petrus Joubert, in Natal, who was sixty-eight, or Piet Cronje, who was sixty-four, had been used all their lives to handling commandos which numbered hundreds. Now their armies were tens of thousands strong. They had been used to skirmishes; now they had to fight pitched battles. At the very beginning of the war, when their best hope lay in riding hard for the sea, they were sluggish, and the defensive tempted them.

Yet, in their first actions against the British, in Natal and elsewhere, the Boers clearly had the upper hand. They defeated the British again and again in the field, but such local victories were not decisive. Boer superiority in weapons and fighting men could not last much longer. Only one strategy could win this war. The Boer commandos must stream down into Cape Colony and Natal, arming their Boer blood brothers as they went, all riding hard for the coast. They needed to deny ports like Durban and Cape Town to the British Army Corps which was still on the high seas. A seaborne landing is the hardest military manoeuvre troops can be called upon to perform, and the British Army

Corps steaming out from England was certainly not equipped to attempt it. Then would be the right moment to negotiate a peace.

But, though the young men urged them on, the old generals' highest desires were set on winning a few small battles. In their hearts they hoped the British did not mean this time to crush the Boers, but would negotiate and compromise and give way, as they always had before.

Though the power of the British Empire, then at its height, could undoubtedly crush the Boer republics when fully brought to bear, the British, when war at last arrived in South Africa, were ludicrously slow off the mark, overconfident and ill-prepared.

Campaigns in the past fifty years, against backward races, had accustomed the British Army to warfare in which masses of ill-armed opponents were brought down by volleys of rifle fire from British soldiers closed up, shoulder to shoulder, in a formation not much different from that of Waterloo. This close-order volley fire might tear holes in the ranks of men armed only with spears, but, to Boer riflemen, British troops in parade-ground order were merely a splendid target. British marksmanship, moreover, was so neglected that on the average an infantryman fired off only three hundred cartridges a year in practice shooting – and this was often done standing up, aiming at a fixed target.

British officers were usually the sons of wealthy men, since, in most regiments, an officer needed a private income, as well as his pay, to meet his mess bills. As regimental officers they were gallant, gentlemanly, and courageous – always ready to lead their men, from in front, against unpromising odds. Soldiers would usually follow such officers anywhere.

But when British officers rose in their profession, leaving their regiments to take general command, working from the map and leading from the rear, these gallant gentlemen often lacked professional military knowledge. They could lead small numbers of men with confidence and courage, but large numbers confused them. The skill and mobility of a well-armed and mounted foe like the Boers led them into outrageous blunders. Men serving in the ranks, who took the brunt of high-ranking officers' mistakes, began as a result to mistrust their own high command. One German critic described the British Army in a significantly bitter phrase, 'Lions led by donkeys'.

In one short week – Black Week – from 10 to 17 December 1899, the British were spectacularly defeated three times. In the long run, however, Black Week transformed the British Army into a force capable of fighting a modern war. They learned from the Boers, and began, in time, to excel them at their own game.

Down through the passes of Drakensberg rode old General Joubert's commandos, some dressed for the occasion in the black frock coats they wore to church. All were bearded, all wore slouch hats, carried Mauser rifles and rode hardy veld ponies. 'Christ is our commander in chief,' Paul Kruger had declared. Their saying was 'God and the Mauser'. In a week, they had cleared upper Natal, and then they faltered.

Serving with the Boer Army were several groups of foreign volunteers – a few hundred Germans, a corps of Dutchmen from Holland numbering 250, and an Irish Corps, mainly Irish-Americans, also about 250 strong, who marched into action under a green flag displaying the Harp of Tara. On their western front, near the diamond town of Kimberley, the Boers also had a Scandinavian Corps, numbering 80. Some of these foreigners were mercenaries, but most were men who sympathized with the Boer cause or, for some political reason, hated the British.

There were some foreign friends on the British side, too. One squadron of South African Horse, for example, was made up of American volunteers, mainly from Texas.

North of the Tugela River, in Natal, the most important rail junction was called Ladysmith. A British general who knew his business would have abandoned it and withdrawn his army southwards, to protect the ports. Lieutenant-General Sir George White, bald, moustached, chronically optimistic, had only been in Natal a few weeks. He allowed himself and his army to be cut off at Ladysmith, a town exceptionally hard to defend since it was dominated by a ring of high hills from which the Boers could shell the corrugated-iron-roofed houses below.

General Joubert took no advantage of this error of judgement. He could have swept past Ladysmith and reached Durban; there was nothing to stop him. But, instead of leaving a small force to contain Ladysmith, precious weeks were frittered away on a full-scale siege. Meanwhile, the Army Corps sent out from England was coming closer.

Cecil Rhodes, after the disgrace of the Jameson Raid, had busied himself chiefly in his new 'empire', now called Rhodesia, north of the Limpopo River, in Matabeleland and Mashonaland. But he knew that Kimberley diamonds were the original source of his wealth and power. To Rhodes, the defence of Kimberley appeared as the war's most important objective. When Cronje's army got bogged down besieging Kimberley, Rhodes made the telegraph lines to important people in army and government buzz with his appeals. One might think this war was being fought especially for the sake of the great diamond monopoly.

Rhodes had arranged for guns and rifles to be sent to Kimberley, and he arrived there himself, on almost the last train, as the Boer army under Cronje cut the town off from the south. Here, too, the Boers embarked on a siege, when they might have moved down fast into the Cape, where forty thousand men of their own background and opinions were waiting to join them.

The eight Maxim guns Rhodes sent to Kimberley were mounted on great piles of debris from the diamond mines – natural forts, which dominated the country around the town. Two thousand armed diggers formed themselves into a volunteer defence corps. Daily, after dark, a great searchlight moved to and fro across the sky, a sword of light, which, for miles to the southward, indicated that the city was still in British hands.

Old Cronje, who as the Boer's Native Commissioner had won a name among Africans for pitiless harshness, dug his men in on both banks of the Modder River, which any British Army coming to relieve Kimberley must cross. Beyond the river, Cronje dug a second set of entrenchments and gunpits, at Magersfontein.

Lord Methuen, the British general coming up to dislodge Cronje, was fifty-four, and had seen service fifteen years before, when he commanded a small unit of irregular horse in Bechuanaland. Since Lord Methuen drew his supplies up the long and vulnerable railway from Cape Town, a bold cavalry leader would have begun the Boers' campaign not by digging in but by riding south, cutting the railway and raising support in the countryside all the way to the Cape. But, under old Cronje, Boer tactics on the western front were even more sluggishly defensive than in Natal.

Lord Methuen advanced with an army of ten thousand men, foot, horse and guns, to the Boer entrenchments at the Modder River. Cronje had pushed forward the men in whom he had least confidence so that, if they felt tempted to run, they would find a river at their backs. Methuen's advance, through triple lines of gunpits and into the unfamiliar crossfire of Boer pom-poms, was costly. A tenth of his force became casualties. Lord Methuen, however, forced the Modder River – only to find, once he had crossed, that the entrenchments through which his men had so bloodily fought their way were but Cronje's outer lines. Ahead lay cunningly fortified Magersfontein – a skilful network of trenches and barbed wire blocking the way to Kimberley.

Tantalizingly, each night, above the heads of Cronje's Boers, the tall, bright searchlight from Kimberley flickered up and down the sky, like a distress signal.

Methuen knew that reinforcements would be needed. Soon, into Lord Methuen's camp marched the Highland

Brigade: battalions of the Black Watch, the Gordons, the Seaforths and the Highland Light Infantry, swinging along gallantly behind their pipers. Some were to find that kilts might be all very well in the Highlands, but not on the high veld. Highlanders, after lying prone for hours in the sun, squinting over rifle sights, would find the back of their legs agonizingly sunburned.

Late on Sunday, 10 December 1899, the splendid soldiers of the Highland Brigade marched out of Methuen's camp, northwards. Their orders were simple: to clear a path for the army through the Magersfontein lines. Their rest in camp had been brief. There were no tents. It had been raining hard, and two soldiers had to share one blanket. As the Highlanders marched off to their night attack, it was still raining.

To maintain his men's marching order in the pitch-darkness and the driving rain, their officer commanding, Brigadier-General A. J. Wauchope, ordered his four battalions to form quarter column. The Highlanders closed up into a solid mass of men. When they marched off blindly into that thick night, their leaders had only the dimmest notion of how and where the enemy would be entrenched. The Highlanders had no scouts, and no flankers. They were, in fact, marching blind, through utter darkness. The Black Watch led the way.

A man in front tripped over a wire. Two dangling tin cans clinked. This was the signal. They were held, blinded and deafened, in a murderous crossfire. Though their brigadier did not know it, the Highland Brigade had already blundered into the midst of the enemy. The first volley struck six hundred men to the ground.

Some Highlanders ran, only to be caught on the barbed wire, where their bodies were found next morning, riddled with shot, and hung up blackly, like carrion crow.

The British guns which had followed the Highland Brigade, to support their attack, heard rifle fire ahead, and unlimbered. The gunners loaded with shrapnel – shells filled with hundreds of lead balls – and opened fire. But they had misjudged the range. More shrapnel fell on the Highlanders than on the Boers.

Only one and a half companies of the Black Watch survived, and Brigadier-General Wauchope was dead. When the remnants of the Highland Brigade were extricated, the night ambush at Magersfontein was found to have cost 1,000 men, including 700 Highlanders, and 57 of their officers.

Magersfontein was the first disaster of Black Week. The second happened, almost at the same time, at Stormberg.

On 1 November, the Boers had begun their leisurely invasion of Cape Colony. If they had started a fortnight sooner and pushed briskly for the sea, Cape Town might have been denied to the British. But General Sir John French – one of the few British generals to improve his reputation in this war – handled his cavalry effectively. Though the Boers took Colesberg, which seventy years before had been the trekkers' rendezvous, they got no further on that sector of the front.

Eastwards, towards the Basutoland border, the British defences were based on Stormberg.

The general commanding here was Sir W. Gatacre – nicknamed by his men General Back-Acher. He had seen fighting in the Sudan, but against warriors in chain mail, armed with spears. General Gatacre was restless and irritable, a thin, square-shouldered figure. He had the gaunt face of a Don Quixote and an enormous chin, not compensated for by any expanse of forehead. His nickname gives him away. 'Back-Acher' is not what a private soldier would call someone for whom he felt respect as a considerate and intelligent leader of men.

When the Boers drove him back from Stormberg to Sterksstroom, General Gatacre decided that he would make a night attack to recover lost ground. Every living soul in his camp knew of this intended attack, two days before it happened. In fact, the war correspondent of *The Times* sent accurate details of it off, in advance, to his newspaper. Since the countryside around Stormberg was friendly to the Boers, they must certainly have known, too.

The day before this attack, when a general less nervously restless – less of a Back-Acher – would have let his men relax, General Gatacre sent one of the units out on an exhausting field day, and kept the rest busy with fatigue chores. Gatacre started his night attack with three thousand men who were falling asleep on their feet.

The general led them into the darkness on horseback. They began to stumble across country that got rough and rocky. General Gatacre dismounted and led his horse, but did not send out flankers or scouts, to see if this broken country hid an ambush. He had already marched farther than his own plan called for, yet on he went. In plain words, General Gatacre was lost.

At 4.15 A.M. the eastern sky became light with the onset of dawn. There he was, energetically leading his horse onwards, with thousands of men marching behind, dropping from weariness.

The Boers had dug rifle pits along the face of a steep hill beside the trail the British were bound to use. They opened up an accurate fire at close range. Gatacre's guns, following behind the troops, unlimbered, loaded and returned the enemy's fire. But the range had been misjudged, and the British infantry were bombarded with shrapnel from their own guns. About a hundred men were killed or wounded, and six hundred prisoners had been taken by the Boers, as well as two British guns. The high proportion of prisoners reveals the truth: the British private soldier, traditionally prepared to fight with blind courage behind officers he knows and trusts, had begun to lose confidence in the way he was being led.

The third disaster of Black Week – at Colenso, in Natal on 15 December – was also caused by bad generalship, but curiously the general concerned, Sir Redvers Buller, never entirely lost his popularity with his men. Large, portly, slow-moving, Sir Redvers Buller's great pleasure was food, and he always saw to it that his men were well fed, too. Nearly twenty years had passed since Sir Redvers Buller won his reputation for bravery as a major fighting the Zulus. Now he had to lead an army.

Though General Joubert had bottled up in Ladysmith the bulk of the British troops originally meant to defend Natal, large reinforcements were now landing. Buller advanced on the Tugela River with 21,000 men at his command. He had infantrymen and a cavalry division under Lord Dundonald, which included the Texans of the South African Light Horse. He had thirty pieces of field artillery and sixteen naval guns, including two 4·7-inch monsters.

'Wait,' men had said knowingly, as the bad news of Black Week started coming in, 'until Buller moves.' The Boers defending Ladysmith had dug in along the banks of the Tugela, but Buller's army handsomely outnumbered them.

A change, however, had come over warfare since the far-off days when the unimaginative fighting generals on both sides in this war had heard their first shots fired in anger.

A Mauser in the hands of a Boer struck death up to a mile. A Boer commando could cover country at three or four times the pace of British light infantry. Modern artillery could shell with precision at a range of several miles. In short, all the distances and proportions with which a commanding general had to reckon were greatly changed from the days when a musket had an effective range of a hundred yards, and you held your fire until you saw the whites of the enemy's eyes.

Moreover, accurate long-range magazine rifles and weapons like the newly invented Maxim machine gun, gave a great advantage to the defensive. Troops who dug in could be further protected by the barbed wire that had begun lately to be used for fencing on veld farms. Attackers would need to outnumber defenders by at least three to one – and many would die in the attempt. This knowledge tempted the

Boers – even at a time when their best hope lay in the offensive – to sit tight, dig in, save lives and let the British make costly frontal attacks.

Colenso was a proof of all this.

On 2 November 1899, the telegraph to Ladysmith had gone dead. The city was surrounded. On 10 November, the Boers reached Colenso, which commanded the railway bridge across the Tugela River southwards. Since the Boers expected one day to cross this bridge, on their own advance to the coast, they did not blow it up. They dug in along the line of the river.

Buller's plan for forcing the Tugela and advancing to relieve Ladysmith looked well enough on paper. One brigade would make an attack, upstream, at a ford called Bridle Drift. They would cross the river, and outflank the Boer trenches on the far bank. Meanwhile the main British attack would have developed at the bridge itself. Once that bridge was taken, the army could get safely across the Tugela, and Ladysmith would be within striking distance.

Bad scouting made nonsense of Sir Redvers Buller's plan. The ford called Bridle Drift was not at the place where the general sent his men to find it. Moreover, the place upstream where the British were sent to cross was at a loop in the river, exposed on three sides to Boer shrapnel and rifle fire.

The brigade sent to Bridle Drift was sent into the attack in close formation. Shoulder to shoulder they went forward, into a hail of bullets, as though on the parade ground. By the time a few survivors reached the riverbank, all order was lost, and six hundred men had fallen. The soldiers who thought they had got to Bridle Drift found no footing in the swift, rain-swollen Tugela, and were swept away.

General Buller's flank attack had come to nothing.

His frontal attack at the bridge itself began to develop in a more encouraging and scientific fashion. The leading brigade advanced in open order – columns of half-companies, extended to six paces. So that the hidden Boer marksmen would lack targets, the little groups of khaki-clad soldiers advanced skilfully, in short alternate rushes over the bare, bullet-swept plain – dropping to take cover, jumping up to run forward with fixed bayonets. The foremost British soldiers had already reached the bridge, and, when that bridge was crossed, the army could follow.

These infantry knew their job, but they were robbed of victory by some nameless artillery officer who had not yet learned how the scale of distances on the battlefield had changed. He sent two batteries of 15-pounder field guns galloping towards the enemy, with no infantry in support. The guns began to unlimber only 500 yards from the Boer lines. Now, any British soldier within 500 yards of a Boer with a Mauser was dead. The gunners dropped around the guns. In the body of one dead man, later, were counted sixty-five distinct bullet wounds.

Out there, in no-man's-land, were twelve field guns, ranged in due order, and surrounded by tumbled corpses. Looking at them made the British general forget what the battle was all about.

His job was to force a passage across the Tugela River. The way to save those guns was to win the battle. His own riflemen commanded those abandoned guns as completely as did the Boers. It would be as deadly for a Boer to lay a hand on those guns as for a Briton to go to their rescue.

Yet the British went on trying to save their dozen 15-pounders. Volunteers ran out to certain death. One of them, an aide-de-camp of General Buller, was the only son of old Lord Roberts, soon to become British commander in chief. The battle turned into a shambles. No one, in fact, could get near those guns, and live.

At last, when his losses in the entire action amounted to eleven hundred men, Sir Redvers Buller abandoned the twelve guns and withdrew on 15 December, having failed in all he had planned.

Although his large, impassive face gave no sign of it, Buller's nerve was shaken. Warfare in which the attacker must pay such a gruesomely high price to reach and overcome an entrenched defender was new to him. In the Zulu War, where he had gained his military reputation, it had been warriors armed with assegais who died in heaps before the fire of modern British guns.

In this one week of 1889 – from 10 December to 17 December – after these three disastrous actions, at Magersfontein, Stormberg and Colenso, the British lost three thousand men and twelve guns. But they also lost some of their complacency. The Boers had twisted the British lion's tail. Now, they must risk his claws.

In London, important decisions were made. One Army Corps would evidently not be enough to drive the Boers back to their capital cities of Bloemfontein and Pretoria. One new division of regular troops was at once dispatched to South Africa, another was formed, and volunteer forces began to be raised and trained in all parts of the empire. It would still, however, they decided in London, be a white man's war. The magnificent Indian Army, though expert in this sort of fighting, would stay at home, in India.

Men of British stock, all over the world, could ride a horse and fire a gun as well as any Boer. Many volunteers were tough frontiersmen from Australia and Canada. The ranks of the Imperial Yeomanry were filled with crack shots and hardriding fox hunters from the English countryside, some supplying their own equipment and refusing all pay. In one single London club, three hundred members volunteered to serve against the Boers. This was, as someone wryly observed afterwards, the last 'gentleman's war'. Before modern weapons of horror were developed, war had an element of adventure.

5

Escape to Freedom

THE ship which had brought Sir Redvers Buller to South
Africa in October had also carried a plump young man of
twenty-five, with something of a soldier about him. He, too,
still thought of war as a chance for glorious adventures, and
he had already seen more war than most of the professional
soldiers on board – bloody campaigns on the northwest
frontier of India, and in Cuba as well as in the Sudan, where
he had ridden in a famous charge at the battle of Omdurman. Though trained as an officer, he had given up the
army to become a writer. His father had been an English
lord, his mother was American-born and known for her
great beauty. He was going to South Africa as war correspondent of the London *Morning Post* – and his name
was Winston Churchill. Though, as war correspondent, he
would technically be a noncombatant, Churchill hoped
somehow to take part in the fighting.

While the big ship wrote her white wake across the
tropical sea, Winston Churchill was impatient. In the days
before radio, a ship could be at sea for weeks at a time, cut
off completely from the outside world – and news of this war
was his business.

Sir Redvers Buller, however, as he sat a long time over his
excellent dinners, looked calm and confident throughout the
voyage. But this was before Black Week – before the elaborate
plans Buller had discussed in London with the government
for a quick British victory were shattered. The British Army
Corps now on the high seas was to be scattered all over the
map – to defend Natal, protect the Cape, relieve Ladysmith,

relieve Kimberley – instead of being grouped for one decisive blow.

Estcourt, upcountry in Natal, was a quiet little township of single-story houses forty miles from Ladysmith. Even so, from that distance Winston Churchill could clearly see that the besieged town was still managing to hold out. To the Boers' astonishment, Captain Tilney, inside Ladysmith, had sent an observation balloon into the air. There it floated, a tiny brown shape on the horizon. The sight of that balloon was tantalizing. Churchill's job was to take any chance that offered to get closer, and see for himself what actually was happening over there.

Blocking the way to Ladysmith were about twelve thousand Boers, outnumbering local troops at this time by six to one. Only a handful of trained troops remained in Natal, but every civilian there between sixteen and fifty was volunteering to help Britain. Men carrying rifles rode in every day from outlying farms, and in a wonderfully short time, these pioneers were learning to wheel and manoeuvre, and fight as irregular cavalry.

Every day some of these cavalrymen went on a reconnaissance of a dozen miles towards the Boer positions, to spot what the enemy might be up to. There were twenty-five youngsters on bicycles, rifle slung over shoulder, who would pedal up the country roads until they caught a glimpse of slouch-hatted, bearded Boers. Then they would race back to report how close the enemy had come.

Young Churchill itched to follow them towards the enemy line. One afternoon his chance came. The men in the railway workshops had built an armoured train. Protecting the sides of the boxcars were bullet-proof steel plates, with slits cut in them for loopholes. The armoured train also mounted one ancient seven-pounder muzzle-loader, landed from H.M.S. *Terrible*. It looked powerful and imposing, but soldiers have a sound instinct – and they named the train 'The Death Trap'.

Churchill accepted an invitation to go up the line towards Ladysmith, in The Death Trap, on reconnaissance.

For the first hour northwards, all was peaceful. The locomotive puffed cautiously over the grassy plain. As a hill went by about six hundred yards to the left, the soldiers peeping through their loopholes saw Boer heads pop up above the crest – bearded, in slouch hats, aiming rifles. Three enemy cannon opened fire – two field guns, and a Maxim quick-firer.

Now the steel plate protecting the armoured train, although proof against bullets, would crush like cardboard if hit by a shell. Hearing the first enemy shell burst overhead, the engineers went into reverse at full speed. It was exactly what the Boers had hoped for.

A group of them had been hiding around the curve, to roll a big boulder on the track down which the armoured train was now reversing. The end of the train crashed into the boulder so violently that one truck was thrown right off the rails. The next truck wedged itself sideways, blocking the way. The train could neither advance nor go back. It was trapped and helpless.

The British soldiers behind those steel slits had, by now, a pretty good idea what to do if it came to the worst. Already the troops had learned that the Boers treated their prisoners well. 'They were the most good-hearted enemy I ever fought against,' wrote Winston Churchill later. 'To the Boer mind, the destruction of a white man's life, even in war, was a lamentable and shocking event.' Take a handkerchief from your cuff, wave it in token surrender – and the rest of the war would be passed up in Pretoria, in a prison camp. Much better than dying heroically in The Death Trap. Men who did this were known, a little contemptuously, as 'hands-uppers'.

Already, as Winston Churchill ran along the line, the white handkerchiefs were fluttering at the loopholes. Boer marksmen, firing as they ran, had begun to close in. Churchill, at the wedged truck, called for volunteers to shift it by brute force, and get the train moving. He had no business doing this. He was legally a noncombatant, a journalist. He should have stood by, and watched.

A heroic shove from the willing hands got the jammed truck clear. Churchill could see two men in civilian clothes coming rapidly towards him. He thought at first they might be platelayers from the breakdown gang which the armoured train carried. But they were carrying Mauser rifles. He too, without so much as waving his handkerchief, had become a prisoner.

His captor was called Louis Botha, a big, jovial, intelligent-looking young Boer who could have taken high rank in the Boer army or government. But Botha had opposed Kruger's ultimatum, believing the tiny republics should never have embarked on a war they could scarcely hope to win. He then joined the ranks as a burgher – a private soldier riding in a front-line commando. The ambush of the armoured train had been Louis Botha's idea.

Not long after this, Botha was appointed commander in chief of the Boer forces around Ladysmith – from private soldier to army commander in a few months. Later he became Prime Minister of South Africa, just as Winston Churchill became Prime Minister of Great Britain. But now they were two young men confronting each other – one a bearded rifleman, the other a dishevelled war correspondent loudly claiming his rights as a noncombatant, though inwardly not very hopeful.

'I'll send word to General Joubert,' said Louis Botha amiably, 'though it isn't every day we capture the son of a lord.'

Young Churchill was then sent to be interrogated by Jan Smuts, a small, slim, fair-haired Boer of about his own age. Smuts was the son of a Boer farmer in Cape Province, and though dressed and armed like the men around him, he had worked his way through Cambridge University, and been

Kruger's Attorney General. He was now doing intelligence work.

With a twinkle in his blue eyes, Jan Smuts heard the captured young Briton's protests about his noncombatant status, and promised to convey them to General Joubert. Then, with the quiet pointedness of a trained lawyer, Smuts began to ask probing questions.

What was a civilian doing, half in uniform and half out, giving orders to troops to clear a railroad track? What had happened to the pistol Churchill evidently had been carrying in the holster strapped to his belt? Churchill, who had no right to bear arms, had, in fact, dropped his pistol by accident. Knowing he had no business out in the front line, seeking adventure, Churchill sought the best arguments he could in reply to this formidable interrogator. What neither then knew was that Smuts, like Botha, would one day also become South Africa's Prime Minister, and a British Field Marshal into the bargain.

When Churchill arrived there, Pretoria, capital of the Transvaal – the city where Africans were not allowed on the pavement, but must run in the gutter – was full of armed riflemen on their way to join the armies, as well as volunteers come out to help the Boers from all over the world. The Boer Minister of War was himself Portuguese. Though the United States had declared herself willing to look after British interests in the Transvaal, the American consul there, Mr Macrum, openly supported the Boers, and was unfriendly to the British held prisoner. French journalists wrote with undisguised delight of Churchill's capture. It was as if the civilized world had decided that Britain's deliberate throttling of the two little republics was unjust.

About sixty captive officers were held in the State Model Schools, under a guard of forty armed police, (called Zarps, from the initials, in Afrikaans, of their proper title: South African Republic Police). The Zarps slept under canvas in the grounds of the school, which were always brilliantly lit with overhead electric lamps. The officers lived inside, in a dormitory. The Zarps kept their weapons in their tents, and, as Churchill soon discovered, the young officers held prisoner were already planning to seize them, and make trouble.

A mile and a half away, on Pretoria Race Course, were 2,000 other prisoners, under the rank of officer, some of them 'hands-uppers', some not. These were held by a guard of 120 Zarps, who relied mostly on two machine guns to keep their captives in awe.

What, then, was to stop the young officer-prisoners from overpowering the dozen Zarps who stood guard over them at any one time? In that tent outside there was a stock of arms. Before an alarm was given, the sixty armed officers might easily reach the race course. Capture the machine guns. Set free the other prisoners. And then – what an opportunity! Sixty trained officers, commanding two thousand troops, in the heart of the enemy's capital!

For the first two days, this plan was discussed in excited whispers. But at last, to Churchill's disappointment, the senior officers overruled it. Everything depended on disarming that handful of Zarps, who stood guard over them night and day, and that was not so easy as it looked.

Once the plan for a breakout was squashed, Churchill decided to make his own escape. The Boers who caught him had never found the money he carried – £75. Three days before Christmas, on 22 December 1899, he 'borrowed' the slouch hat of the clergyman who had come for the Sunday service, and got over the wall when the guard's attention was distracted. He wore a dark suit of civilian clothes, and had four bars of chocolate in his pocket, as well as the money. His plan was to reach the Portuguese frontier, 280 miles away, by travelling down the railway line to Delagoa Bay. Though dressed more or less like a Boer, Churchill knew not one word of Afrikaans or any of the native tongues. There were armed Boer patrols everywhere. He would have to use his wits.

The Delagoa Bay railway ran northwards out of Pretoria,

winding its way into the hills. Each bridge was guarded, which meant young Churchill had to detour, stumbling his way across unknown country. After dark, he hid in a ditch near a small station, and listened for a train.

With a glow and a snort, a freight train approached. Churchill caught a brief glimpse of the engineer's face, red-lit by the furnace. As a freight car rattled by, he jumped for it, grabbing upward. He found a handhold, clung on, and clambered aboard. The car contained empty coal sacks. Churchill burrowed among them and slept, while, at twenty miles an hour, the train trundled through the night.

In the small hours, Churchill woke. To be safe, he must get off this train before daylight. He got from under the dirty, gritty coal sacks, and went to squat on the couplings, picking his moment to jump. He made giant strides through the air, and landed in a ditch, unhurt. Dawn was coming up. On the skyline, beside a ravine, was a grove of trees. Churchill hid among the trees, and wondered what to do next.

Though the night had been cold, when the sun came up the heat grew oppressive. Overhead circled a huge *aasvogel*, the South African vulture. It lives on carrion, and can always be seen over battlefields and other scenes of disaster.

In the distance was a Kaffir kraal. These were beehive-shaped huts of wicker, smeared with sun-dried mud, amid gardens of corn and beans, with a separate kraal of thorn nearby for the cattle. Fifty yards off was a spring. But, thirsty though he was, Churchill dare not go down there, nor even throw himself on the mercy of the natives, who, since they hated the Boers, would sometimes favour an Englishman. He was trapped in that grove of trees by two armed Boers who strolled to and fro at a distance, occasionally taking potshots at birds. All day Churchill lay there, thirstily, amid the trees, in the growing heat, watching the railway line. Three trains went by, and he observed them carefully.

The trains went slowly up a gradient, and even more slowly around the curve beyond. At that curve, it might be possible to climb aboard a moving train with no one seeing.

After dark, Churchill made his way up the track, and waited. waited. No trains came. He began, impatiently, to walk the rails, in the general direction of the Portuguese frontier. Still no trains. At each bridge, he had to leave the track, and circle at a discreet distance, to avoid the armed guards on sentry.

Coming to a station down the line, he found there the three trains which had passed the grove of trees during the day. All three were run into a siding. To climb into a stationary freight car would be easy enough, but suppose, instead of heading for the frontier, it pulled back to Pretoria? Churchill heard two Africans laughing. Then a voice, speaking Afrikaans, gave them a harsh order. He moved away from the dark station quickly.

Two or three bright fires gleamed a long way down the track. Thinking they might be cooking fires from a kraal, Churchill decided to take his chance on the Africans there agreeing to hide him from the Boers. Perhaps, if they understood the value of money, they might even let him pay them for a pony and a guide.

But, walking slowly in the darkness towards the bright glow, he found they came not from fires in a Kaffir kraal but from the furnaces of steam engines which worked the winding gear at some coal pits. Nearby was a small stone dwelling.

Would the man who lived there be Boer or uitlander? Might he take a bribe?

Churchill decided to knock. A light appeared in the window.

A voice asked, in Afrikaans, '*Wer ist da?*' But the man who opened the door spoke in English. 'What do you want?'

Boer? Or uitlander? He might be either.

Churchill decided to be cautious.

'I'm a burgher,' he replied, 'joining my commando – but I've had an accident. Fell off a train – I've been unconscious for hours . . .'

'Come in,' said the stranger. He took Churchill through the doorway to an office. The man locked the door.

To someone recently a prisoner, a locked door is always

ominous. Yet there was something about this man which suggested that he might not, after all, be a Boer.

'I think,' said Churchill, 'I had better tell you the truth.'

The stranger said slowly, 'I think you had.'

'I am Winston Churchill. I am making my way to the frontier. Will you help me?'

A pause – a dubious silence. All at once, the man was smiling, giving Churchill his hand. 'Thank God you've come here. It's the only house for miles where you'd be safe.'

The colliery manager, though an Englishman by birth, was a naturalized citizen of the Transvaal. Word was out, he said, of Churchill's escape. The whole country was looking for him, and posters had been put up with his portrait offering a reward for his capture, dead or alive.

'Give me a pistol, a pony and a guide, and I'll make my own way to the coast,' Churchill offered. But this was not so easy. There were two Boer servants, actually sleeping in the house. The Africans employed around the mine would notice any stranger's face, and might be tempted by the reward.

'We'll have to hide you in the mine itself.'

At dawn, Churchill was taken quickly across to the cage under the winding gear, and lowered into the mine. All was pitch-dark. He was led by winds and turns to a disused part of the mine, and left there on an old mattress, with a few candles, a bottle of whisky and some cigars. There would be a long wait.

Food? Those servant girls might notice if food disappeared, and ask awkward questions. It would have to come later. Churchill fell into a sound sleep. When he awoke, he felt around in the darkness for the candles.

They had disappeared. He was there in total darkness.

At last, a moving light indicated the approach of the colliery manager. He brought a cold chicken with him. The disappearance of the candles made him laugh. 'The rats,' he said, 'must have eaten them.'

There, in the circle of light cast by the lantern, watching

Churchill out of their little pink eyes while he ate his breakfast, were hundreds of rats. He chewed the chicken; they bared their little sharp teeth.

The waiting, day after day, seemed endless.

'The hue and cry,' said the mine manager, 'is dying down at last.' The Boers, having lost all trace of Winston Churchill, had begun to believe he must still be hiding somewhere close to Pretoria. The time had come to risk the last stage of the escape.

A load of wool was going down to Delagoa Bay on the 19th of January. This wool, packed in large, square bales, would fill three railway trucks. In one of these trucks, the bales were to be arranged to leave a concealed space, long enough to lie in, wide enough to sit up in. There the fugitive could hide. At two in the morning, Churchill followed the mine manager to the waiting truck, and slipped into his prearranged hiding place amid the bales of wool. There he found supplies: two roast chickens, a loaf of bread, three bottles of cold tea. Through a chink an eighth of an inch wide, he could look on the outside world as if through a keyhole.

During his long wait in the mine, Churchill had learned by heart the names of stations through which the train would pass on its way to the coast: Witbank, Middelburg, Bergendal, Dalmanutha, Machadodorp and, at long last, Komatipoort, on the frontier between the Transvaal and Portuguese territory, where the danger would be greatest. Whenever the train was to stop in a station, Churchill decided to force himself to stay awake, for fear a snore might betray his hiding place.

Late the next afternoon, the train reached Komatipoort. Churchill lay down flat and covered himself with sacks, so that even if the frontier guards looked in, they might not notice him. His heart was beating with excitement. The train stood still on the track. Three or four hours passed, and the excitement faded. Nothing happened. Darkness had come, and, helplessly, he fell asleep!

Churchill awakened with a start to find the train standing still once more. Did this mean they had passed the frontier? Had anyone heard him snore? Later, the train began to move. In another station, it stopped. Looking out through his tiny spyhole, Churchill saw men in Portuguese uniform. On a signboard was the name Resana Garcia. He had crossed the frontier – and nothing could stop him now.

Winston Churchill got back, at last, to the British lines, to find that his daring escape had made him famous. However, during the time he had been on the run, Black Week had occurred: disaster after disaster, at Magersfontein, Stormberg and Colenso.

The defeat at Colenso was only the first of the military blunders with which the name of Sir Redvers Buller was to be identified in the coming months. At Colenso, the big, ponderous, grunting general had not only lost 1,100 men, he had also lost his nerve, though the younger officers around him did not yet know this.

Buller had sent a panic telegram to London: I DO NOT THINK I AM STRONG ENOUGH TO RELIEVE WHITE. To Sir George White himself – the bald-headed, moustached, over-optimistic soldier who had let himself be trapped in Ladysmith, but was now defending the place with dogged courage – Buller sent orders to fire off all his ammunition, and make the best terms he could for surrender. White sent a cold reply, to say he had no intention of surrendering. The London government sent Buller an even colder cabled message: IF YOU CANNOT RELIEVE LADYSMITH, HAND OVER YOUR COMMAND TO SIR FRANCIS CLERY, AND RETURN HOME.

When Winston Churchill rejoined him, however, Sir Redvers Buller, by keeping an impassive exterior and replying to anxious questions with grunts and knowing looks, had got his nerve back. It might have been better for the thousands of common soldiers, who in the next few months were to die in his repeatedly bungled attempts to relieve Ladysmith, if Buller had admitted his fallibility, and gone.

The Germans at one time had pretended a warm friendship for the little Boer republics, and had encouraged them in their defiance. But so far, in this war, they had not committed themselves officially to either side.

Outright alliance with the Boers would mean the enmity of Britain, and this was a price the Kaiser was not yet prepared to pay, though Germany had supplied the Boers with arms and advisers.

In fact, though his people might sympathize with the Boers – as, indeed, most people did – the German Kaiser was at present trying to keep friends with both sides. He was closely related by blood to Queen Victoria of England. To her personally, through the British Military Attaché in Berlin, he sent a curious message:

'I cannot sit on the safety valve forever. My people demand intervention. You must get a victory. I advise you to send out Lord Roberts and Lord Kitchener.'

In the long run, the foreign friends whom the Boers had trusted were to prove two-faced. Except for the help given them by a couple of thousand foreign volunteers, including some Americans, and even a few Englishmen who sympathized with the justice of their cause, the Boers were to fight a long and terrible war alone.

6

B-P in Mafeking

MAFEKING is a small township in Bechuanaland, on the railway north from Kimberley to Bulawayo in Rhodesia. The town lies uncomfortably close to the Transvaal border, and a small place nearby, Pitsani, had been used by the Jameson Raiders as their headquarters.

To the west of Mafeking extends the broad and pitiless Kalahari Desert; to the east stretch the arid grasslands of the Transvaal, but through Mafeking itself trickles a small river, the Malopo. North and south, in a straight line, runs the railway. Mafeking is, militarily speaking, a town hard to defend, on the edge of nowhere – a town which can be isolated from the outside world simply by cutting, to north and south, the railway line which brought it into being.

Mafeking, when the war began, in October 1899, was simply a frontier settlement of no special importance, a cluster of houses with hardboard walls and corrugated iron roofs, a church, a race course. If the Boers wished to take Mafeking, what was to stop them?

The British, when war threatened, could spare no regular troops to defend the place. They sent there, instead, a hand-picked group of younger officers, with instructions to organize some sort of defence and hold the Boers up for as long as possible. A cavalry colonel named Baden-Powell was put in command. He was later known all over the world by his initials B-P, and became famous as the founder of the Boy Scouts.

Colonel Baden-Powell had served in Rhodesia against the Matabele a few years before. Scouting – moving off from the main body of the army, like a huntsman, to seek out a way ahead, and keep a watch on the foe – was a form of warfare in which the Matabele excelled. But B-P would glide off into the night on his rubber-soled tennis shoes and beat them at their own game. Though he was a soldier who later was to rise to the head of his profession, as Inspector General of Cavalry, B-P had about him a great deal of the impudent, irrepressible, astoundingly clever schoolboy. He conducted the defence of Mafeking as if it were a tremendous lark, a school field day, from which, at evening, all would go home, tired out but good friends, to eat strawberries for tea.

Even before war was actually declared, the Boers began massing their commandos on the border opposite Mafeking. B-P and his little group of brother officers had managed, by then, to muster about 900 riflemen, including 179 police, 340 irregulars of the Protectorate Regiment and 200 volunteers. All men in the town, like storekeepers or businessmen, who had other jobs to do but were capable of bearing arms, formed themselves into the Town Guard. The Africans, dreading the Boers, were glad to help the British in their preparations. Led by a rich South African contractor called Benjamin Weil, everyone went cheerfully to work fortifying the town.

People in Mafeking learned that they were being led by a man who understood clearly the type of war he would be up against. Rifle fire from scientifically designed entrenchments and bomb-proof forts covered all the approaches to the town. When a bullet-proof screen was needed to protect the hospital, it was quickly improvised by erecting two big sheets of corrugated iron four inches apart, and filling the gap with gravel. Since the long, straight streets could be swept by enemy snipers, the ends were screened off with sacking. Outlying dugouts were connected with headquarters not by a runner, who might or might not arrive with his message, but by that new-fangled invention the telephone, which B-P regarded as a marvellous new toy.

All field telephones ran into his bomb-proof headquarters, over which B-P built an observation platform, which he called the Conning Tower, high enough for him to survey the whole town and everything around it. He could therefore control the defence of any endangered sector by picking up a telephone and giving an order. This order might, as likely as not, be given in the form of a bad pun or a high-spirited joke.

Apart from their rifles, the British had two small seven-pounder field guns and six machine guns. They also came across an ancient muzzle-loader, dating from the Napoleonic Wars, which they christened 'Lord Nelson'. They mounted it on a homemade gun carriage, and learned to fire 'Lord Nelson' by carefully studying the boys' adventure stories of Captain Marryat which were so popular in nineteenth-century England.

B-P gave one strict order. His men were to shoot off their precious cartridges only at enemy targets they were sure they could hit. Once all the cartridges were gone, the defence of Mafeking would be finished.

Two more field guns were expected from Cape Town, but the authorities had been slow in dispatching them. They came up by a train which, on 12 October 1899, was derailed by Boer raiders forty miles to the south. The link to the outside world was cut. From that moment, the siege was on. Month by month, men, women and children in Mafeking would watch the grass grow green and wither over the railway line that led southwards to freedom.

The next day, on 13 October, the Boer commandos which had been poised at the frontier pounced on Mafeking – five thousand mounted riflemen, led by that shrewd veteran, Piet Cronje. The Boers had reason to expect a quick victory. What earthly hope had the British of holding an open town, on a plain, attacked by a force of crack shots who outnumbered the amateur defenders by eight to one?

The advancing commandos drove back the pickets, which B-P had moved towards the frontier, to keep his foe under observation. Out from town, to help the retreating pickets, steamed an armoured train, supported by a squadron of the

Protectorate Regiment. They drove the Boer advance guard back.

Fresh reinforcements were pouring across from the Transvaal, and at one moment it seemed as if the squadron and the armoured train might be cut off and surrounded. Dashing out from Mafeking to their rescue came a second tiny force, two troops of horsemen and one small seven-pounder. Between them, they kept the enemy at bay with a shrapnel bombardment until their comrades could withdraw to safety. A risky business – the siege of Mafeking could have come to an end in those few moments if Baden-Powell's small-scale counter-attack had failed. But it was a success, and it gave the Boers a foretaste of the military dash, or call it schoolboy impudence, with which the defence of Mafeking was henceforth to be conducted.

On 16 October 1899, the siege began in deadly earnest. The Boers brought up their Krupp guns, sixteen-pounders, which outranged the two small field guns defending Mafeking. They captured the town's water supply (but B-P, aware it could not easily be defended, had already dug wells). He had also anticipated the Boer shelling. The town was controlled by a system of warning bells, so that the defenders in any given sector could take cover when there was actual imminent danger, but get back to work in the fairly safe intervals.

General Cronje sent a message to the officer commanding the defence of Mafeking, calling on him to surrender to avoid bloodshed.

'And when,' asked Colonel Baden-Powell gravely, 'is the bloodshed going to begin?'

This was the last exchange between the two commanders for some time. After several weeks of persistent shelling, however, B-P decided that he, too, could play the message-sending game. He sent formal word to Cronje that, if the shelling of Mafeking went on any longer (it had never stopped, day or night) he would be obliged to regard it as amounting to a declaration of war.

This schoolboy nerve – not even a good joke, perhaps – was simply part of the original Boy Scout's innermost nature. But such impertinent good spirits had a tonic effect, in putting the hopelessly outnumbered defenders on their toes. As they smiled at B-P's jokes, they forgot the odds against them.

Baden-Powell had to hold a perimeter of five to six miles with a force which, counting in the Town Guard, amounted to only twelve hundred men. But those British riflemen, sitting behind loopholes in trenches which covered every approach to the town, had already taught the Boers clearly that an all-out assault on Mafeking would cost them more lives than the place would be worth. In sober fact, considering the strategy of the war as a whole, Mafeking was worth little or nothing to either side. It was a sideshow, though the Boers were tying up, at Mafeking, men and guns which might have tipped the balance in their favour on some more decisive front. But Mafeking, even if unimportant in the grand strategy of this war, remained a thorn in their side.

Cronje sent for one of the four huge guns which the Boers had shipped in from the French cannon foundry of Le Creusot. Over and over again this Creusot gun dropped on Mafeking a 96-pound shell, which could demolish an entire house. Since Mafeking's two 7-pounders were too weak to make any sort of reply, B-P decided on a sortie.

After dark on 27 October, a hundred men lined up to hear the quiet orders of Captain FitzClarence, who was to command the attack. No firing – the Boers were to be taken by surprise, and fought only with the bayonet they so much dreaded.

The Boers surrounding the big Creusot gun, never expecting an attack, were dozing in trenches they had covered by tarpaulin because of the persistent rain. When the British roared up at them, yelling in the dark, and began prodding them out of cover with cold steel, the Boers panicked. Some, pulling down the tarpaulin, got entangled within it. Others grabbed their Mausers and fired, but hit their own men.

79

Though seven of the British were killed and the Creusot gun soon resumed its bombardment, this sortie taught the Boers that the siege of Mafeking was not merely to be a safe, monotonous shelling of a helpless civilian foe.

A small hill inside Mafeking's defence perimeter, called Cannon Kopje, where the field guns were mounted, was defended by Colonel Walford, of the British South African Police, and fifty-three policemen. It was clear to General Cronje that if he could take Cannon Kopje, all Mafeking would be spread out before him and at his mercy. The bearded Boer riflemen moved in on Cannon Kopje in great force, only to learn what the British elsewhere in South Africa were painfully discovering: a few good riflemen, well dug in, could hold off a massive attack. No Boer soldier could put a living foot on the parapet of the British trenches. Each one of the defenders would have taken four or five Boers with him before Cannon Kopje could be overwhelmed. The attackers, having lost heavily, drew off. The British, in this decisive action, lost six killed and five wounded.

The Boer high command had never counted on an army of five thousand riflemen being tied up at Mafeking. Knowing now the mettle of these obstinate opponents, General Cronje handed over operations to Commandant Snyman, who was left with two thousand men, and orders to maintain a strict blockade. Cronje himself went south, with the rest of his force, to deal with Lord Methuen on the Modder River.

On 3 November, and again on 7 November, the British, as if to keep the new commandant on his toes, organized sallies against this blockade, each of which hit the Boers where they least expected. On 18 November, Baden-Powell sent his compliments to Commander Snyman, and impudently informed him that he could not expect to take the town of Mafeking just by looking at it. To the two thousand Boer soldiers dug in around him, B-P sent a personal message, advising them to stop fighting, and go home to their families. It did the morale of the defence no harm that their com-

(*Top*) Major-General Kitchener
(*National Portrait Gallery*)
(*Above*) General De Wet
(*The Mansell Collection*)

(*Top*) General Louis Botha
(*Illustrated London News*)
(*Above*) Colonel Baden-Powell
(*Illustrated London News*)

(*Top*) Cecil Rhodes
(*National Portrait Gallery*)
(*Above*) President Steyn
(*Illustrated London News*)

(*Top*) President Kruger
(*Kruger House Museum*)
(*Above*) General Smuts
(*National Portrait Gallery*)

(*Top*) An armoured train at the siege of Ladysmith (*The Mansell Collection*)

(*Above*) The Devons' charge on Wagon Hill at the siege of Ladysmith (*The Mansell Collection*)

(*Above*) British troops at Modder River in Black Week (*The Mansell Collection*)

(*Right*) A piper leads the Argyll and Sutherland Highlanders into an ambush at Magersfontein (*The Mansell Collection*)

(*Left*) British Mounted Yeomanry (*Imperial War Museum*)

(*Centre*) A captured Boer Krupp gun (*Imperial War Museum*)

(*Below*) Colt machine-gun and galloping carriage. A Red Cross wagon on the left (*Imperial War Museum*)

(*Top Left*) British troops learn Boer tactics (*Imperial War Museum*)

(*Top Right*) Gordon Highlanders with a heliograph (*Imperial War Museum*)

(*Left*) Building a bridge (*Imperial War Museum*)

(*Above*) A military reconnaissance balloon (*Imperial War Museum*)

(*Top*) A Boer and his sons off to war (*Illustrated London News*)

(*Above*) General Cronje surrenders to Field-Marshal Lord Roberts at Paardeburg (*The Mansell Collection*)

(*Top*) British prisoners at Pretoria. Winston Churchill is on the right (*Radio Times Hulton Picture Library*)

(*Above Left*) Boer prisoners await transportation to a prisoner-of-war camp (*Imperial War Museum*)

(*Below Left*) Boer women and children flee Kitchener's 'scorched earth' (*Imperial War Museum*) mander spoke and acted, from the very start, as if victory were a foregone conclusion.

Snyman was less chivalrous to the British than General Cronje had been, and was no less brutal to any Africans who got in his way. He started deliberately to shell the women's laager – a safe compound, where the besieged women and children were known to take shelter. So B-P put all his Boer prisoners in there, too, and they got their share of the shelling.

Occasional little victories kept up British morale inside the town, but on the day after Christmas, came disaster.

To the north of the town, the Boers had mounted a troublesome gun. B-P planned a sortie to put this gun out of action – a large-scale operation involving both his field guns, and eighty of his best men.

Somehow, the Boers got word this raid was coming. Hastily they strengthened their defences, so that an attacking force would get nowhere unless they brought up scaling ladders, and climbed them under a hail of point-blank rifle fire.

Watching from the Conning Tower, B-P soon knew that something had gone seriously wrong. On the open ground around the Boer fort, he could see a scatter of dead and wounded khaki-clad bodies, which got thicker as the crackle of rifle fire from the hidden Boer riflemen grew louder. Out of the eighty attackers, fifty-four had already fallen when B-P, tears misting his eyes, shut up the telescope with a snap, and said, wearily, 'Let the ambulance go out.'

Even Commandant Snyman, when it came to burying the dead and bringing in the wounded, showed a touch of the chivalry on which the Boers traditionally prided themselves when fighting a 'Christian foe'. Snyman was a devout Calvinist, so on Sundays there was no sniping, or bombardment either. (Though he warned the British that if they persisted in playing cricket on the Sabbath, he might be compelled to shell them.) The outermost trenches had crept so close to each other that in some places no-man's land was only fifty yards wide. On Sundays, when the firing stopped, Boer and Britisher who all week had been trying hard to kill each other would exchange chit chat and jokes, and even gifts.

The sector of the five-mile perimeter around Mafeking which the Boers controlled least effectively was that confronting the Kalahari Desert. Slipping through here, once in a while would come 'postmen', bringing letters for the garrison and news to B-P of how the war elsewhere was going.

The news was encouraging. B-P's bold and brilliant defence of Mafeking, in a war which everywhere else had been marked by British incompetence and disaster, was making the little township into a symbol of far greater importance than its actual military value. Two British forces might in due time relieve Mafeking.

To the south, at the far end of those grass-grown railway lines, Lord Methuen was still not far from Kimberley. Though hurled back with great loss from Cronje's entrenchments at Magersfontein, he had dug himself in on the Modder River, and, when reinforced, could be expected to move north again. Down from Rhodesia, southwards, was moving a gallant little contingent under Colonel Plumer, numbering upward of seven hundred men. They were restoring the railway line as they came, and making their way slowly down it, headed by an armoured train.

At times, the defenders noticed men and guns being taken from the Boer blockade, to go north and hold Plumer back. When they returned, news of the relieving force would drift across the narrow space between the lines. Secret messengers, expert at scouting across vast African distances, would come and go between the beleagured garrison and Plumer's slowly advancing railhead. But the distances cutting off Mafeking from the nearest help were still immense. All the defenders knew they would have to hold out a long time yet.

Inside the town, organization, initiative and imagination were doing wonders. The Mafeking railway workshops had become a little ordnance factory, where two engineers from the Locomotive Department and a sergeant of police turned out shells. They found a pile of useless 5-pounder shells left over from the Jameson Raid. These they cunningly adapted to fit their own 7-pounder gun.

The Locomotive Department's greatest triumph was Mafeking's answer to the Creusot Long Tom, the Boer 96-pounder which daily blew large holes in the fabric of their community. The engineers and the policeman managed to make a gun of their own. It was a strange piece of artillery – a smoothbore which fired a 5·5-inch round shell. But the homemade big gun threw its shell with great accuracy a long way, and gave the Boers the surprise of their lives when it first opened fire.

Trench systems on both sides had now crept so close that homemade hand grenades could be thrown. The cricket-playing English excelled at this dangerous game. Sergeant Page, of the Protectorate Regiment, an expert fisherman, developed a method of which he, alone, was the master. He cast his grenades into the enemy trenches with rod and line. The British riflemen, under stress of war, were becoming such crack shots that the enemy's Creusot gun had again and again to be moved farther from the town, as the men serving it came under fire from British snipers. The moral initiative lay with the outnumbered and hungry British.

Though food was running low – people had been experimenting with toasted locusts and cooked rawhide – B-P decided to celebrate an official Day of Jubilee. Anything would be a relief to break the monotony of loud bangs and sudden death.

The day began with a cricket match. There were organized athletic sports in the afternoon. In the evening, the bachelor officers were to give a concert in Headquarters, followed by a dance. Colonel Baden-Powell himself came down from his Conning Tower long enough to sing a much-applauded comic song. The ball, however, did not proceed quite as planned. There was one inconveniently long interval when the men on the dance floor had to run for their rifles and move off to repel a Boer attack. But since the ladies were waiting, they came back later, to finish the programme as planned.

The six-month anniversary of the siege was celebrated by a billiard tournament. The billiard tables were still miraculously intact, though the saloon had had several holes knocked in it by shells.

On other fronts, the war by now was not going so well for the Boers. To encourage their lukewarm friends overseas, it had become politically important to the Boer leaders that they should achieve an emphatic success. Since the whole world now knew how amazingly Mafeking was holding out, a Boer victory at Mafeking would echo around the globe. From his Conning Tower, B-P took note of what the men slinging their homemade hand grenades in the trenches had already begun to observe. Boer reinforcements were arriving.

Mafeking had been a thorn in the side of the Boers for too long. The obstinate defence of this little border town, though not vital at first to the war's strategy, was beginning to turn the scale along the entire northwestern front. It hampered any invasion of Rhodesia, and encouraged the Africans in Bechuanaland to stay loyal to the British. Most of all, Mafeking was a symbol – a well-known place on the map, where the Boers might still win a propaganda victory.

On Saturday, 12 May 1900, when the siege was seven months old, the Boers attacked Mafeking at dawn. Three hundred picked men, under Commandant Eloff, had crept around during the night to the less well defended sector of the town facing the desert. They rushed the native quarter, and set the huts there afire.

The Protectorate Regiment had their barracks nearby, connected to B-P's Conning Tower by field telephone. Colonel Hore, and twenty officers and men were in the barracks when the Boers led by Commandant Eloff took it by assault. Eloff, who possessed his own sense of humour, took the telephone off the hook to advise Colonel Baden-Powell in person that his barracks had been captured.

But B-P, now the sun was up, could see that for himself. The possibility of this attack had been in his mind for a long time. He had already decided how it should be met. The weakest part of a line is a temptation to the enemy. If he chooses to break through at what apparently is the point of least resistance, he may be lured into a trap. This happened now.

The Boers swept down to capture a stone kraal within the British lines, and then to occupy a low hill, as B-P had anticipated they would. Once inside the British perimeter, they could take cover behind the walls of the barracks and the stone kraal. But now they could neither advance further in, nor retreat. The British, from shrewdly planned entrenchments, were surrounding them with a crossfire which caught every living thing that moved out of cover. Escape was a deadly impossibility.

By seven that evening, Commandant Eloff's men, having fought all through the hot day, had emptied their water bottles. A force under cover with the three indispensables – food, water, cartridges – could resist indefinitely. Without water, Eloff knew the game was up. He and 117 men of his force had been trapped. He flew the white flag, and the Boers around him laid down their arms, after ten of their number had been killed and nineteen wounded by the rifle fire which so skilfully kept them penned in. Among the prisoners were Dutch, French and Germans who had volunteered to help the Boer cause and hoped to figure in the propaganda victory.

Baden-Powell had the prisoners brought to see him. 'Good evening, Commandant,' he said to Eloff cheerfully. 'Won't you come in and have some dinner?' He gave the prisoners the best supper the township could supply. His chivalry was mixed with cunning. When the Boers across the lines got to hear this, they would think the British in Mafeking were still not badly off for food.

Colonel Plumer's relieving force was daily coming closer. In the May days that followed Eloff's capture, help also crept towards Mafeking from the south. The bloody battle of Paardeberg had by now been fought and won. A relieving force numbering twelve thousand mounted men, accompanied by horse artillery, was moving up from Kimberley. By 15 May, they had reached Mabisi Stadt, twenty miles west of Mafeking. Here their commanding officer, Colonel Mahon, kept a rendezvous with Colonel Plumer, who from the heart of the continent had come the long way south. They combined forces, and moved on to the relief of Mafeking, down the Malopo River.

Commandant Snyman's outlying Boers were driven back from a water supply they hoped to prevent the relieving force from using. They retired towards the trenches at the east of Mafeking, outgunned and outnumbered. Here B-P played the last cheerfully optimistic card in the long game of bluff and counterbluff, which was ending now in victory for the gallant handful of British defenders. He led his men out in one last brave sally against the Boers, and saw them driven, dispirited, out of their trenches.

Once the Boers had begun to move out, their retreat went on. Soon there were no signs that Mafeking had ever been besieged, except for the gaunt faces of the hungry defenders, the holes in the houses, and, on the eastern horizon, a long smudge of dust, where ox wagons were rolling back to Pretoria.

When the siege of Mafeking began, each rifleman had 600 cartridges. So well had the ammunition been husbanded through seven long months of endless fighting that, when relief came, the cartridges remaining averaged out to 120 to each rifle. In those days, when the rifle dominated the battlefield, Mafeking could have held out even longer.

Of the 900 irregular riflemen who had defended the township, 273, or nearly a third, were killed, wounded or missing.

7

A Case of Complete Surrender

THE most famous living British soldier was a very short, grey-haired man, with broad shoulders and an extremely straight back, who had won his first reputation nearly fifty years before, in the Indian Mutiny. His title was Lord Roberts, but to the man in the street and the private soldier in the ranks, he was universally known as 'Bobs'.

A man nicknamed Bobs is likely to be good-natured. Lord Roberts not only cared for the everyday comfort of his men, but in time of war would rather use his brains to save their lives than batter his way through an enemy position by brute force.

When Lord Roberts heard that his only son had been killed at Colenso, he went at once to the Secretary of State for War, and told him frankly what the Kaiser had already told Queen Victoria – that the Boers might even win unless there were a radical change in Britain's supreme command.

The word was passed to the Prime Minister, Lord Salisbury, who at sixty-nine was near the end of his political career, and well aware of it.

'If Lord Roberts has himself in mind – he is too old,' declared Lord Salisbury. Roberts was sixty-seven. However, his great reputation rested on a solid basis of past victories, in Afghanistan and elsewhere. Who else was there to call on?

'Lord Roberts may go as Commander in Chief,' said the Prime Minister at last, 'providing he takes Lord Kitchener of Khartoum as his chief of staff.' Kitchener, twenty years younger, had recently built a great reputation commanding the Egyptian Army which had conquered the Sudan at the battle of Omdurman, when sixty thousand men in chain mail, armed with swords and spears, fell prey to the field guns and automatic weapons of a highly trained modern army twenty thousand strong. Kitchener's nickname, 'K of K', sounded uncommonly like the cocking of a gun. A man called K of K may be efficient, but is hardly likely to be loved.

Kitchener was a tall, dark man, straight as a lance, his brutal mouth hidden by a heavy moustache, his complexion burned to a strange, almost purple, hue. His eyes, too, were odd. Bright blue, with a slight squint, they appeared never to be perfectly in focus. Kitchener, who never married, was a tireless worker. Having done three hours work before breakfast, he would go on until late at night. A capable organizer, he liked to keep in his own hands all the strings of power.

Whereas a modern general has a staff of picked and highly trained officers working to bring the men, munitions and supplies to battle at the right moment, Kitchener preferred to do all such work himself. This was only in part from love of authority. Kitchener mistrusted, and rightly, the brave but amateur officers in the British Army, who served the Queen because it was a social fashion and neglected the boring details of their profession.

Kitchener had a vein of bizarre cruelty in him, too. After one Sudanese battle he had dragged the defeated Emir through a nearby town in chains, with a halter around his neck, being whipped as he went. After the battle of Omdurman, Kitchener dug up the bones of the Mahdi, the Sudanese religious leader who had opposed him. He carried the Mahdi's skull round with him in a kerosene can, and made jokes about using it for a drinking cup.

Such conduct is more like that of an oriental potentate than a traditional English gentleman. Many brother officers in the army mistrusted and disliked Kitchener, though everyone agreed he was remarkably efficient. Others came under the powerful charm of his strong personality, and would go to their deaths for him.

Kitchener's unusual upbringing had shaped his outlook on life. His father, a retired colonel who went to live in Ireland, never looked upon the Irish as anything but hewers of wood and drawers of water. Kitchener kept this attitude to 'lesser breeds' all his life. His father, however, had been eccentric to the point of lunacy. Because he did not believe in using blankets, he made his wife sleep under newspapers, until her lungs were affected, and she died. One day, young Kitchener was pegged out on the lawn as a punishment, lashed to croquet hoops, staring up at the sun in an attitude of crucifixion. Did he consider such behaviour cruel – or normal?

A man with a background like this was one of the two men on whom the British Government now relied to crush the Boers. Curiously enough, Kitchener and Roberts, so dissimilar in character, worked together well. Roberts made the plans, Kitchener saw that they were carried out.

When Roberts and Kitchener landed in Cape Town on 10 January 1900 – midsummer in South Africa – their strategy was decided. Sir Alfred Milner, who as British High Commissioner was a civilian with a ringside seat, called it, and rightly, the only *strategy* of the war.

The Boers could be beaten in the field only if they were heavily outnumbered. This meant moving masses of men and supplies over the vast high plains of South Africa, and concentrating them for an attack. The army, therefore, must be supplied from a port by a railway. The obvious one to use, starting on the coast from East London and Port Elizabeth, led into the heart of the Boer republics by more or less following the old Trekkers' Road. This was the direction in which the Boers would expect an attack.

But there was another railway, longer and more exposed, leading from Cape Town around the western flank of the republics, then going north through besieged Kimberley to Mafeking and beyond. Cronje's victorious army lay across it, entrenched near Magersfontein, beyond the Modder River.

If Cronje could be pushed out of the way, a back door, so to speak, would open into the Orange Free State, and thereafter, the Transvaal. Boer commandos now dominating northern Natal, or pushing against the British cavalry screen to threaten Cape Colony, would have to turn their horses' heads around, and scamper back to defend their homes. Bloemfontein and Pretoria, the enemy capitals, would be in striking distance of the British army. Once they were taken, surely the war would be won.

To manoeuvre Cronje out of his entrenchments at Magersfontein, surprise was essential, and surprise meant secrecy and speed.

Kitchener, at his desk from six in the morning until late at night, began in his bold, legible handwriting to issue a stream of curt, immediate, lucid orders, to set the British army in motion. Grouping it powerfully again, he skilfully moved his troops in a way that kept the enemy guessing. His plan was to concentrate, by February, near the Modder River, a force of 37,000 men, 113 guns, 12,000 horses, and 22,000 transport animals – but all so poised that the Boers could never be certain in what direction this army would ultimately strike.

Rhodes, in Kimberley, was still making a nuisance of himself, trying to run the siege – trying, indeed, to run the war. Kitchener sent word to Colonel Kekewich, the infantry officer commanding the defence of Kimberley, to put Cecil Rhodes under arrest if necessary.

Another strong man had arrived in Africa.

Lord Roberts, by a simple but brilliantly skilful manoeuvre, completely misled the Boer general, Cronje, and got his cavalry division across the Modder River. The British cavalry under General French were galloping hell-for-leather, now, to relieve Kimberley. They arrived there on 15 February. Cronje was ill at ease to know they were in his rear. Meanwhile, British mounted infantry, foot and guns, numbering tens of thousands, after misleading Cronje by a skilful feint, began to move on his left flank, and threaten his line of communications.

Piet Cronje recognized the danger. Abandoning his entrenchments at Magersfontein, he began to move as fast as he could along the north bank of the river, towards his base at Bloemfontein. The British infantry and guns began racing for Klip Drift, hoping to cross the Modder River northwards, and block Cronje's way. Now they had Cronje in the open, they wanted to bring him to battle.

All had gone according to plan, except for one counterstroke. A Boer leader called Christiaan De Wet – a foxy-faced little farmer with a genius for guerrilla war – who had been sent by Cronje with a commando of 1,000 men into the British rear, had pounced on their supply train. Kitchener's careful planning might have got all his men and supplies to the right place at the right time. But for the next month, thanks to De Wet, his army would have to march and fight on half rations.

The parallel movement of the two armies along the north and south banks of the Modder River was a race of life and death – a contest between an army of farmers, plodding at the pace of the oxen which drew their wagons, and an army of hungry and thirsty regular soldiers, route-marching under the devastating sun, who so far in this war had not seen their generals win a battle.

Cronje had 5,000 men. Some were with their wives and children, because in the past few months that fortified camp at Magersfontein had seemed a safe place. If Cronje had been younger and more ruthless and the leader of a disciplined professional army, he would no doubt at this moment have abandoned all those wagons, to move his men along the north bank of the Modder fast, on horseback. He could then have turned about when and where he chose, to oppose the British advance on Bloemfontein.

But Cronje, though tough and shrewd, was slow. The younger men around him, and the trained German volunteers he sometimes asked for advice, might urge him to abandon the wagons. But Cronje knew that the trek wagons which served as his army transport were the personal property of men in his commandos, and valuable property. Those 5,000 mounted riflemen, therefore, were obliged to walk their ponies along the riverbank at the pace of oxen, two or three miles an hour. They were less an army than a people on the move.

Even so, the Boers, starting at dusk the night before, managed to slip through the gap between the rear of the British cavalry, galloping off to Ladysmith, and the vanguard of the marching division under General Kelly-Kenny. Next morning, from the dust cloud raised by their wagon train, Kitchener could see that Cronje had already gone past Klip Drift, and was moving to cross the Modder River farther on, at Vendutie Drift.

Kitchener at once sent a mounted messenger – a galloper – with orders to General French at Kimberley, to turn about and ride to the next ford but one beyond Vendutie, called Koodoo's Drift, and head off Piet Cronje there.

General French did not receive his orders to block Koodoo's Drift until ten o'clock on the night of 16 February – after a day which had been the hottest of the South African summer. French warned Kitchener that his cavalry were exhausted – and so they were. Of the complete division of men which had made the mad dash to relieve Kimberley, only 1,500 men and 12 guns were fit to move. But French promised to get them moving.

The exhausted cavalrymen were roused from their sleep in the middle of the night. They tightened girths on their weary chargers, and were once more in the saddle. By four in the morning, the remnants of the British cavalry were drawn up in column, ready to start the gruelling 30-mile ride to Koodoo's Drift. French drove weary men and weary horses hard, and got them there in six and a half hours. He arrived at the Modder River on the morning of the seventeenth, at half past ten, with several small Boer commandoes clinging to his flanks, to cut off stragglers and pounce on any false move.

Vendutie Drift was in sight, four and a half miles to the westward. General French saw Cronje's men had already begun to cross the river there. He at once ordered his horse-artillery to drag their guns to high ground, and open fire. Shells began to explode at Vendutie Drift as the leading wagons went lurching thirty feet down the steep bank, to cross the fifty-yard-wide, shallow, muddy river, and climb the bank on the south side.

The roar and stink of exploding shrapnel sent white water up in splashes of high spray. The draft oxen stampeded, many were killed – and the shelling brought the wagon train to a halt. The pace of the British cavalry, footsore though it was, had proved faster than the pace of the ox. Since Cronje could neither move forward nor back, he dug in where he was.

This, anyway, was traditional Boer fighting – in a laager – the form of warfare that had served them well seventy years ago, against the Matabele. Cronje knew he was out-numbered seven to one. Digging in and staying on the defensive would reduce these unfavourable odds.

The huge laager, which the five thousand farmers and their strapping womenfolk, spade in hand, began then and there to build under the hectic shellfire from Koodoo's Drift, enclosed the entire ford at Vendutie, north and south. The Modder River providing water for man and beast ran through its centre. The banks of the river were thickly covered with a growth of mimosa, thorn and other scrub – dry and spiky now in midsummer, but excellent cover. The plain of dried grass beyond, across which the British would be obliged to attack, was exposed and bare. For at least half a mile in every direction, Boer rifle fire could dominate.

Many ravines on both sides of the river ran down to the ford, making natural trenches. The Boers laboured with pick and shovel to improve and connect them. From the moment the shelling started, all through that long, hot day, and all night under the bright stars, they dug and shovelled. Faster than Kitchener would believe possible, they dug out a complete system of connected trenches, hidden by scrub bushes, which gave them a field of fire commanding every approach to Vendutie Drift.

In the river's deep banks, they excavated dugouts, where the women and children could take shelter from bullet and shrapnel. In a small red house to the north of the ford, Cronje set up his headquarters. Behind him, protected by a ring of entrenchments, was the Krupp gun which was the Boer's chief piece of artillery.

Cronje had seen British soldiers defeated more than once before. However, even after the disasters of Black Week, he was not inclined to underestimate his enemy. He saw that they had come against him now in vast masses – red-necked, khaki-clad soldiers in their big sun helmets, who marched across the veld in heavy boots, and were willing to make up in blind courage for the professional ineptness of their officers.

This time however, Cronje observed, there had been no ineptness whatever about the way the British troops had been handled. They had turned up, like magic, on his vulnerable flank. Their cavalry had made a dash to Kimberley and back at a pace which no Boer commando could have excelled. They had skilfully blocked Vendutie Ford with their artillery. A change, evidently, had come over the British.

Cronje sat there under his broad-brimmed hat in the little red house, and issued orders in a slow voice that never increased in tempo, whatever the danger. As he thought out and ordered his tactical dispositions, he would stroke his beard from time to time, or put fingers under his hat to scratch his head, like a farmer pondering the price of cattle. Cronje knew there were three points in his favour.

The first was the folly of British generals, which up to now had always cancelled out the courage of their men. This time the British had done well so far, but there was still time for their usual crass blunder. That might give him his chance to break out.

Secondly, De Wet's thousand men, and other commandos, too, were operating out there on the veld, across the enemy's lines of communication. To feed and supply such a vast body of men as the British had now brought against him would need an enormous flow of ammunition and food. A British general who felt his supplies threatened would surely move even more slowly than usual, and perhaps stop in his tracks.

Cronje also believed, mistakenly, that the British had no firm intention of fighting to a finish. Before, they had always struck a bargain – patched up a peace. They were white men, too, after all. And the Boers' foreign friends, the Germans, or perhaps the Americans, might even now be bringing pressure to bear on the British Government in London to come to terms and end the war.

Cronje was by nature obstinate. His decision was to make a long resistance – patiently to exact the highest price in time and lives from the British, and slow down their advance towards Bloemfontein. Meanwhile, luck might change.

Lord Roberts, the grey-haired, broad-shouldered little fighting man with the back straight as a ramrod, was feeling his age. When the British Army moved off, he had stayed behind at Jacobsdal, on the Reit River, kept there by what the doctors diagnosed as a feverish chill. Was Lord Roberts dreading, perhaps, the loss of life that the coming battle would entail? Roberts hated to get his men killed. He thought in terms of feint and manoeuvre and had no love for a bloody head-on encounter.

On 17 February, when the army had almost reached Cronje's laager, he ordered Lord Kitchener to take command.

And command was what Kitchener loved above all things. There was, however, one small difficulty. Though Lord Kitchener had served in a high rank as commander-in-chief of the Egyptian Army, his rank in the British Army was lower than that of French, who led the cavalry, of Kelly-Kenny, who commanded the army's vanguard division, or of Colvile, another divisional general. They were all Lieutenant-Generals. Kitchener was only a Major-General.

Was that so important within a few hours of the most important battle of the war?

Lord Roberts, from his long military experience, knew that it could well be. Any army is based on discipline. The private soldier jumps to obey the sergeant as if his life depends on it. The sergeant moves sharply to the lieutenant's word of command. The lieutenant salutes the major, and carries out his orders at once, without question.

But, as if reacting to so much unquestioning obedience earlier in life, high-ranking officers are often vain and touchy. They stand on their rights, and sometimes need to be coaxed. The simple human explanation is that men with the combination of talents and character which go to form a great – or even a good – general, are extremely rare. But many men who have not been proved in battle attain a general's rank and wear his uniform. War is above all a testing time for generals, and they know it. Conscious that they have to live up to their rank, and justify it, they are jealous of all encroachments. They feel the eye of history upon them.

To the generals who outranked Kitchener, Lord Roberts tactfully wrote, 'I hope to join you tomorrow. Meanwhile, please consider that Lord Kitchener is with you for the purpose of communicating to you my orders, so that there may be no delay.' Kitchener was commanding, therefore, but only as a mouthpiece. The other generals were expected to obey – but they could always fail, somehow, to catch the tones of their master's voice.

Huffily, General Kelly-Kenny replied, in words which, though formally obedient to his commander in chief, show his bitter resentment, 'With regard to my position and Lord Kitchener's, your description of it I perfectly understand. This is not a time to enter into personal matters. Till this phase of the operation is completed, I will submit even to humiliation rather than raise any matter connected with my command.' He could hardly have promised obedience more grudgingly.

Kitchener, who went into bivouac on the night of 17 February with General Hannay's mounted infantry, knew that in the next day's battle he would be singularly on his own. He knew he was not universally loved. The div.sional generals might obey him promptly, or they might quibble and drag their feet. He had, moreover, no means of communicating his orders efficiently on the battlefield, no personal staff of trained officers on whom he could rely. He had a few gallopers, mounted errand boys, who would gallop away briskly with a written message, and perhaps bring back an answer, if they lived. Kitchener decided he would have to chase his army into action tomorrow single-handed, like a sheepdog, scurrying around, snapping at the heels of the flock, to get them all moving in the right direction.

At dawn on 18 February 1900 the tall, heavily moustached general, with the strange, unfocused blue eyes, rode his charger to some high ground nearby, and in the company of a few other officers, inspected the battlefield. Those standing near saw him silently, deliberately, impressively, turn his head from side to side. But how many details of the terrain spread out beneath could the famous commander actually see?

Kitchener was lifting his field glasses now, to scan the Boer laager, and scrutinize more closely the lie of the land. To the British rear stretched the dry, sunburned veld, from which at intervals rose boulder-strewn kopjes. Ahead of them lay the line of the Modder River, marked by its flanking thorn bushes and crossed by the rutted road that led down to the ford. In Cronje's laager, scarcely a Boer could be seen, so well had they dug themselves in. There, under cover of bush and entrenchment, lay five thousand superb marksmen.

During his brief dawn reconnaissance, Kitchener made one serious miscalculation. His experience in warfare had all been against brave but ill-disciplined native foes. He simply did not believe the Boers could have dug themselves in so well, and with a skill in military science which gave their entrenchments a field of fire covering every approach to the ford. The Boers, thought Kitchener that morning, might have built for themselves an inner stronghold, but hardly more.

During the previous night, by pushing out patrols to test enemy resistance, it should have been possible to make sure what the British would be up against. But Kitchener's inclination, now as ever, was to keep all vital information in his own head, and make personal judgements on the evidence – not always first-class evidence – provided by his own eyes.

He was now forming a plan of battle. It would be his own plan, because if he consulted his divisional commanders, who mostly outranked him, the discussion would never end. In fact, even those commanders anxious to fight the way Kitchener wanted were never quite sure how to act, because his battle plan had not been fully confided to them.

First and foremost, Kitchener had to decide whether to attack, or to besiege. Cronje could, in time, be starved out, but waiting for this would give roving commandos longer to strike at the British Army's communications and supplies, and so impose a delay on its programme of advance. Even to Kitchener's eyes, that ford appeared a strong position. To attack it would cost men's lives. But Kitchener, though thrifty in all other respects, never showed deep concern for what, in those days, was called with cheerful cynicism the 'butcher's bill'.

As Lord Kitchener stood there, like a statue, inspecting the enemy positions, an aide-de-camp respectfully tugged his sleeve. The general turned, impatient of being touched. A message was coming from four miles away, clear enough even for those unfocusing eyes.

From French's cavalry position at Koodoo's Drift, a heliograph had begun to wink. This was a mirror mounted on a hinge, which could flash reflected light many miles across the sunlit air of the high veld.

General French's message was plain and glum. His men

and horses were exhausted – and, after their hard riding, no wonder. French, though he could not join in the attack, undertook to block the enemy's road of escape eastwards, and to hold off the commandos that were approaching the field of battle from the north.

'Gentlemen!' said Kitchener impressively to the officers around. 'It is now six thirty. By ten thirty we shall be in possession of the laager; and I shall then load up French, and push him on to Bloemfontein with the cavalry.' His programme for the day expressed a magnificent confidence and perhaps concealed a low opinion of the foe. How was it to be brought to pass?

Kitchener's tactical plan was simple to the point of brutality. Kelly-Kenny's division would make a frontal attack, from the south of the river, at 10 A.M. Meanwhile, Colvile's men were to attack from the east, along both north and south banks, while Hannay's mounted infantry, taking up the job French's cavalry had been unable to shoulder, were to cross the river and attack the laager on the far bank from the west. It was to be a simultaneous attack on all fronts.

Kitchener had no headquarters, virtually no staff, and no machinery for coordinating the three attacks. He had no chain of command. The army was organized so primitively that a battle plan had necessarily also to be simple.

Kitchener had courage and energy, however. He knew that his regimental officers were valiant, and eager to attack, and their troops would follow loyally where they led. Hannay, anyway, had grasped what was expected of him. His mounted infantry had crossed the Modder before dawn, and were now to be seen, working their way towards the laager, to support Colvile's attack from the west, when it became fully developed.

At eight, Kitchener telegraphed to Roberts, still feverish at Jacobsdal, 'I think it must be a case of complete surrender.'

From then on, through the entire day, Kitchener spent his

time galloping at top speed from one side of the battlefield to the other, giving orders by word of mouth. His shouted commands sent one detached unit after another up against the Boer laager, no matter what previous orders they might have received. He hustled troops forward wherever he found them. By midmorning, Kitchener had got his entire army into action. It was a remarkable personal achievement, a notable expression of his physical energy and force of will. But the result was chaos.

The first British troops, as they went forward to attack in open order, revealed in broad daylight what better reconnaissance would have found out more cheaply. For a long way in every direction around their perimeter, Boer marksmen dominated. A British soldier who charged across that field of fire in daylight was dead.

Moreover, detached commandos from Bloemfontein were moving over the edge of the horizon in the British rear. Hannay's mounted infantry already had a Boer commando coming up behind, and, at 10 A.M., it attacked.

Kelly-Kenny's orders had been clear and simple – to make a frontal attack on the laager. Only an all-round attack, supported by every man in Kitchener's command, would have the slightest chance of reaching the Boer lines. But, when he saw Hannay on the far side of the river menaced by this newly arrived commando, Kelly-Kenny detached his 18th Brigade, under T. E. Stephenson, to go and help Hannay.

Kitchener, watching from a distance, was astounded, therefore, to see an entire brigade, which should have been moving east against the foe, abruptly turn west. He sent an aide-de-camp to ask Stephenson what he was about. The aide-de-camp, galloping back on a lathered horse, sought in his mind for some form of words which would express tactfully the snub he had just received. 'Stephenson,' he reported, 'had no clear idea of Kitchener's orders.'

Nor, evidently, had General Kelly-Kenny.

Kitchener again had to gallop in person to the trouble

spot, and there impose his will. He ordered Stephenson to ignore the threat to Hannay's rear, and to go into action against the laager. He then galloped in person to Hannay, and told him French would deal with the attacking commandos. He then sent his senior staff officer to French, telling him to get on with it. But French's own rear was menaced by another commando.

Cronje's riflemen, safe under cover, were managing to hold simultaneous attacks by Colvile from the east, and by Kelly-Kenny from the south. The Mausers rattled incessantly. The helmeted, khaki-clad British soldiers rushed forward in alternate groups, dropped to their faces, jumped to their feet and once more dashed forward. The bodies of those who would never rise again dotted the plain around the laager. The closer to those efficient Boer entrenchments, the more deadly the fire. As the unendurable sun rose up into the sky towards noon, the costly attack continued, but the heart had gone out of it.

Bullets whined around General Kitchener's head as he spurred his charger once more across the firing zone, this time to harangue Colvile, another general who outranked him. Colvile had been leading the attack along both river-banks from the east. This was the attack which, when better developed, the mounted infantry under Hannay were to support from the opposite direction.

'Your attack,' Kitchener told Colvile, 'must be pressed home, regardless of casualties.'

Colvile obediently flung into battle even the men he had left guarding the baggage, only to see, as he did so, that the attack from the other direction, led by Hannay, had already been brought to a standstill.

The three attacks, if all made at the same time, might have brought at least some British troops to the parapet of the outer Boer trenches. In hand-to-hand fighting with the bayonet, the British should have been effective. But so far, despite all Kitchener's furious galloping, this coordination was lacking.

At 1:30 P.M., Kitchener got a note from Hannay to say his mounted infantry could make no further progress. K of K scribbled a characteristic reply. 'Time has come for a final effort. All troops have been warned that the laager must be rushed at all costs. Gallop up, if necessary, and fire into the laager.'

All troops had not, in fact, been 'warned for a final effort at all costs'. Kitchener had no means of warning them, and when Hannay received this reply at 3 P.M., he could see this was so.

Taking Kitchener's harsh words, therefore, as a reflection upon his personal courage, General Hannay shouted to the three officers and fifty men nearest him to mount their horses. Riding at their head, he led them in a futile if gallant charge, directly at the hidden marksmen in their trenches. Hannay fell to the ground, riddled with bullets, and his men died around him, having in the most literal sense obeyed the order of their general commanding. It was a terrible form of protest.

Stephenson's brigade took Hannay's place in the attack from the east, at the same time as Colvile's baggage guard, under Aldworth, made a desperately brave attack from the west. Both were beaten off.

On the battlefield now appeared the master of surprise. Over the afternoon horizon, in the rear of Kelly-Kenny's division, galloped five hundred men under the elusive guerrilla leader, Christiaan De Wet. He led men and guns quickly to the crest of a kopje in the British rear. The troops ironically named it Kitchener's Kopje. Almost before Kelly-Kenny had time to look over his shoulder and notice De Wet's arrival, those Boer riflemen, scattered under cover of the kopje's boulders, were sniping, and Boer guns had begun to spray the disheartened British in the back with shrapnel. The kopje was a natural fortress.

Swearing obscenely, as if his own monumentally impassive reserve had at last broken down, Kitchener sent troops off to attack the kopje. But they were weary and disheartened,

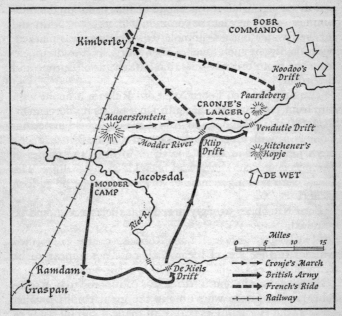

The Battle of Paardeberg

thirsty and lacking sleep. De Wet stayed where he was. Night was falling. Kitchener ordered all troops to dig in at the farthest point they had so far reached – an order that, like so many other orders on this battlefield, did not reach many of them. This order, had it been literally obeyed, would, anyway, have left the most advanced troops exposed next day to Boer fire and sentenced them to death. So, after dusk, even some of those commanders who had been told what to do hastened to disobey and withdrew their forward troops under cover.

Cronje's Boers that night could watch the British soldiers, desperately thirsty, after the heat of the day's battle, creep in ones and twos down to the riverside, to fill their water bottles. Under the stars, they were perfect targets, but the Boers knew vividly enough what it was like to be thirsty out on the mid-summer veld. They let the common soldiers come down and fill their water bottles, unmolested. This war was marked, occasionally, by such touches of chivalry, soon to disappear from the more brutally scientific battlefields of Europe and the world.

The next day, 19 February, Lord Roberts brought with him from Jacobsdal the Seventh Division, as reinforcement. Roberts was well enough to inspect the battlefield in person. Conferring with his generals, he found that the British, in one day's fighting, had lost 1,262 men. Most of the ponies in Cronje's laager, however, had been killed, by shellfire. The Boers were no longer mobile, and could make no sudden escape.

Lord Kitchener strongly urged that the attack should be resumed.

'The laager,' answered Lord Roberts, 'cannot be stormed without further loss of life, which does not appear to be warranted. Let Cronje be starved into surrender.'

Since the war in South Africa was considered to be a dress rehearsal for future wars among the great empire-owning powers, the German General Staff made a careful study of the campaign. In their account of the Battle of Paardeberg, as the attack on the laager was called, they sharply criticized Lord Roberts' decision to call off the attack because of such a consideration as unwillingness to lose soldiers' lives. Coming events cast their shadow.

Nine days after the battle, on 27 February 1900, Cronje surrendered. Little Lord Roberts rode forward with his army to Bloemfontein, the capital of the Orange Free State.

8

Persevere to the End

WHEN an enemy's army has been overwhelmed in battle, and the enemy's capital is occupied by one's own troops, the general commanding has done his duty, and the war is over. The politicians must get on and make a peace. That, as Lord Roberts understood it, was how civilized nations made war. After Cronje surrendered, and Sir Redvers Buller, down in Natal, had finally and clumsily blundered his way into Ladysmith, the way to Bloemfontein, and after, Pretoria, lay open. The war was practically over.

After the shine had been restored to their military reputation by the victory at Paardeberg, the British, thought old Paul Kruger, might after all be willing to leave the Boer republics at least a shadow of their independence. He would yield as much as they wished. The Americans had said they were willing to mediate between Briton and Boer, but Britain refused.

The Boers, however, had one point on which they could not in honour give way. Boer farmers in Natal and Cape Colony, of the same background, speech and religion as the Boers of the fighting republics, had come to the aid of their kinsfolk. Since technically they were British subjects, they were legally rebels and traitors, and the British could hang them all. Kruger knew he could not decently make any peace which did not safeguard the life and liberty of such men.

Milner, therefore, and others like him on the British side, who wanted this war to end with the total extinction of Boer political power – *unconditional surrender* – could delay peace as long as they chose, simply by refusing to discuss pardons for 'traitors'. And the British Prime Minister, Lord Salisbury, was also taking a high and mighty line.

On 5 March 1900 President Kruger of the Transvaal and President Steyn of the Orange Free State telegraphed to Lord Salisbury from Bloemfontein, warning him that '. . . if Her Majesty's Government is determined to destroy the independence of the Republics, there is nothing left to us and our people but to persevere to the end . . . conscious that the God who lighted the inextinguishable fire of the love of freedom in our hearts, and those of our fathers, will not forsake us, but will accomplish his work in us, and our descendants.'

This sounded like a peroration from a long sermon, though in sober fact to 'persevere to the end' was literally what the obstinate Boers intended.

Lord Salisbury well knew that the Boer army, defeated in the field, was melting away, and could never fight another pitched battle against the huge forces Lord Roberts had marched into the middle of Africa. He replied, with a touch of aristocratic hauteur, '. . . the British Empire has been compelled to confront an invasion which has entailed a costly war, and the loss of thousands of precious lives. This great calamity has been the penalty which Great Britain has suffered for having in recent years acquiesced in the existence of the two Republics. . . . Her Majesty's government can only answer Your Honours' telegram by saying that they are not prepared to assent to the independence of either the South African Republic or of the Orange Free State.'

Of the predicament of the 'rebels', not a word.

Bloemfontein was an unimpressive place for a capital city, set in a vast plain of withered grass, with shrub-covered hills to the north. Above the iron roofs of the one-storied brick houses rose conspicuously the government offices. As the British troops moved in, Union Jacks fluttered plentifully, even from the windows of Boers. The British were expected to be lenient. Men who had ridden out to war against them were being told that if they took an oath of neutrality, they could go home to their farms, and get on in peace with the business of raising stock.

The British, after a long stretch – thanks to De Wet – of marching full days on half rations, were a ragged and hungry army. The Guards, for example, Her Majesty's crack troops, and in London a brigade with a reputation for fabulous smartness, marched into Bloemfontein with uniforms so worn that the worst dressed had to be crowded to the inside ranks, where their indecent nakedness would not cause offence. The army had marched its way right through its heavy boots. Ten thousand horses and mules had already died, and the rest of the cavalry mounts were in a bad plight.

Even before Lord Roberts encamped his army, he knew that to make a victorious advance on Pretoria, his men must first be supplied. Essential stores all came eight hundred miles, from base in Cape Town, up a one-track railway which crossed the Orange River over a temporary pontoon bridge. His army was big, but vulnerable.

Lord Roberts was sixty-seven. He rode into Bloemfontein at the head of his troops, small, erect, wearing the staff cap with a broad red band which always seemed too big for him, and with brightly polished brown riding boots but no medals or insignia, though his chest might by rights have been ablaze with them. His bright-blue eyes flamed even brighter than medals would have done – an old man with the heart, if not the energy, of youth. Lord Roberts had been used to commanding in wars that ended in a decent, orderly fashion. If the Boers understood the first thing about war, they would surely now give up.

Enteric fever struck the British Army. This waterborne disease, which kills and enfeebles, was said by the doctors to have come from the bad water at Paardeberg, but in any event it had been prevalent around Bloemfontein for years.

For this reason the disease-breeding wells inside the city were no longer used, and instead a new, hygienic waterworks had been built on the Modder, twenty miles away.

Armies in those days were used to losing more men from disease than from the enemy. A strict order to boil all water might, as the doctors knew, have saved a thousand lives. But sanitary precautions were slack. Seven thousand troops fell sick of enteric fever, and men were dying at the rate of fifty a day. This disease in his army gave Lord Roberts yet one more reason for not pushing north in a hurry.

On 18 March Lord Roberts sent a brigade of mounted men, under Colonel R. G. Broadwood, with two batteries of horse artillery – 9-pounders – eastwards across the plain to make sure of the waterworks. They were at the end of a road, well-worn by wagons and army convoys, midway between the city and Thaba Nchu, or Black Mountain, which had been famous in the Great Trek as a rendezvous, and could be seen from many miles away.

Colonel Broadwood occupied Thaba Nchu, forty miles from the city, and sent Colonel Pilcher, with three cavalry squadrons, another thirty miles farther on, to Ladybrand, to find out what the Boers were up to.

Colonel Pilcher came back with two Boer prisoners. All was well. He had seen a couple of Boer commandos heading north, no doubt to join President Steyn, who was understood to be at Kroonstad, preparing to withdraw into the Transvaal.

What the British did not, as yet, understand was that the Boer Army had been weakened, and yet, in an unusual way, strengthened by defeat. Boers not heart and soul in the war were deciding to take the oath and go home to their farms. But the zealots who remained were the finest patriots. The commandos remaining in the field were smaller but more effective; they were composed of men who had made up their minds to fight 'to the bitter end'.

Colonel Broadwood, hearing that enemy commandos had been seen heading north, began to feel secure at Thaba Nchu.

Then he had second thoughts. With Boers, you never could tell. They covered country so quickly. One Boer name already sent shivers down the backs of senior British officers, that of Christiaan De Wet. Suppose De Wet himself were out there on the loose, somewhere on the veld?

Looking at Thaba Nchu with a tactical eye, Colonel Broadwood could see that, with the mounted brigade at his disposal, it was by no means easy to defend. Urgent word then came that the Boers had wheeled around, and were moving towards him.

The British under Colonel Broadwood retreated across the plain to the waterworks itself, which was surrounded to north and west by broken hills. The next night, two thousand Boers came down out of those hills, and opened fire on the British with several guns.

Colonel Broadwood considered his position carefully. This bombardment was forcing him to withdraw from the waterworks again, and to retreat to Bloemfontein. But already word had been sent to General Colvile's division to come out and relieve him. A whole division could carry out a task that was too much for his brigade. The plain between here and Bloemfontein, though intersected with dongas – deep watercourses with a muddy trickle at the bottom – was constantly in use by British convoys. A glance showed how safe it was.

Posting his cavalry, therefore, in what seemed the danger point – at the rear, where those two thousand Boers from the hills, and their guns, were menacing him – Broadwood sent his wagons and his own guns on ahead. Colvile's strong force, coming out from Bloemfontein to meet him, would only be a few hours away. A ticklish operation was being carried out in a soldierly manner.

But De Wet, who already had robbed the British troops of their initiative by impudently wheeling around to back-track out of the hills and shell them, had prepared a surprise within a surprise. The broad, rutted convoy road dipped down into the largest donga that crossed the plain, and rose again clear on the other side. A wagon crossing that donga would tip down to disappear from sight for a minute or two, then reappear as it lurched up the far bank.

British horsemen, from the rear of the brigade, watched their first wagon come close to the lip of the donga, and go down. After a minute or so, it bobbed into sight again. What was there to worry about?

Only this. Lining the slopes of that donga were three hundred of De Wet's riflemen. They had been waiting where the road dipped down since before dawn.

As the first British wagon, loaded with wounded and carrying a Bantu driver, went down the slope, the Boers seized the driver and put a man of their own in his place. When that wagon reappeared, the British wounded in it were captives.

Wagon after wagon went one by one over the edge, until a hundred had been captured. The 9-pounder guns themselves were very close to the donga, almost in the trap. So far, no warning had been given. But one man, as he went down into the donga, saw armed Boers waiting for him. He had time to draw his revolver and fire a warning before they jumped him.

The Boers showed themselves now, over the rim, a long row of slouch hats, bearded faces, Mauser rifles. From point-blank range they opened fire, as the first battery of horse artillery was teetering at the donga's very edge.

A limbered-up horsedrawn gun is helpless. Five out of six guns in U battery succumbed to De Wet's riflemen, their teams shot down, their gunners captured. The rearmost gun turned and managed to gallop off, followed by four out of six guns from Q battery. Meanwhile the cavalry wheeled away, and re-formed, leaving many horsemen dead behind them on the veld.

A thousand yards off, the surviving guns turned. They un-limbered, to open fire on the Boers with shrapnel shells. But a thousand yards away was too close. A sniper with a Mauser could often kill a man at twice that range, and forty Boer marksmen, quick-firing at a clear target, had a firepower equivalent, it had been estimated, to a direct hit by a small shrapnel shell. Those five British guns were outclassed.

To move forward and rescue their guns – which had made the same mistake here as at Colenso, of engaging too close when dominated by enemy fire – the cavalry dismounted, to form a skirmishing line, and moved forward on foot.

Meanwhile, what was General Colvile doing, with a division of men which, if only it moved up rapidly, could take the Boer ambush between two fires? De Wet's men had all known they were risking their skins in this ambush. Where was Colvile?

General Colvile, hearing the gunfire and morbidly nervous of a Boer trap, was cautiously moving his division off to one flank, out of the way. Meanwhile, his gunner officers, recognizing from the 'section fire' of the beleaguered guns that the case was urgent, fretted and raged at being stopped from going to help their comrades-in-arms.

Broadwood knew he was beaten. De Wet had made that road across the donga a deathtrap. He found another road over the dried watercourse, two miles to the south, and brought his cavalry across there. He had lost three hundred wounded and missing, of whom two hundred had been taken prisoner. The Boers swiftly drove off their loot – a hundred wagons, and seven 9-pounder field guns. The British in Bloemfontein, having lost control of the waterworks, went back to using well water, and the deaths from enteric fever rose.

Against an enemy which could live off the country, ride sixty miles a day, get information and help from every inhabitant, and snipe at you a mile away, it was not enough simply to win battles.

Small commandos that fought as the Boers were now beginning to fight could tie up huge numbers of British troops, who were trained for a more conventional warfare.

This was the painful lesson which Roberts and Kitchener were soon obliged to learn.

The British had already put seven divisions of regular troops into the field. From fortresses and garrisons all over the Empire they scraped together a last division of odds and ends. The Eighth British division were not exactly crack troops. Their general commanding was Sir Leslie Rundle, an officer who had seen service in the Sudan. The troops nicknamed him 'Sir Leisurely Trundle'. To pit a gentleman like Sir Leisurely against a quick-witted guerrilla genius like De Wet was grossly unfair. It helps to account, however, for the way 2,500 Boers under De Wet held up 25,000 British troops for ten days, by mere bluff. This action was at the beginning of the irregular war, when the sieges and pitched battles were over.

Sir Leisurely Trundle's Eighth Division, moving across the hills towards Dewetsdorp, south of Thaba Nchu, found that an unknown number of Boers had dug themselves into the grass ridges that blocked his way into the town. There were in fact only 2,500, but they were commanded by De Wet. Brabazon's cavalry, out in front, exchanged shots with these Boers, and three or four enemy guns opened up, to make a modest skirmish.

That evening, the general himself arrived with two brigades, and made leisurely preparations for an attack on the enemy position some time next day. Since the unnecessary losses at Colenso and Paardeberg, however, Lord Roberts had let it be known that he preferred his generals to win their battles by outflanking manoeuvres rather than by frontal assault.

Sir Leslie Rundle's leading brigadier was Sir Herbert Chermside, an elderly soldier, but an exceptional personage in the British Army, where very few had had modern war experience since the fighting in the Crimea, forty-five years earlier. Sir Herbert, only twenty-two years before, had seen action in the Russo-Turkish war. Asked for his opinion on the

Boer entrenchments, he said they looked as formidable as the position the Turks had fortified at Plevna, Bulgaria. Suddenly Sir Leslie remembered that to take Plevna by assault had cost thousands of lives.

He decided, therefore, to wait for reinforcements. Two brigades of Guards, on the march from the railhead, would arrive under General Barr-Campbell by nightfall. The attack was cancelled. The day was spent in skirmishing.

By evening, Sir Leslie disposed of a force of eleven thousand men and eleven guns. He outnumbered the enemy by more than four to one, a satisfactory superiority. All was put in readiness for a battle next day.

On the veld, fountains and springs are rare. Both sides, therefore, would sometimes find they were going to the same place for water, much as wild animals come down at dusk to share the same waterhole. That evening, forty men of the Berkshire Regiment, going to fill their water bottles, walked innocently into a larger force of Boers, and were surrounded and taken prisoner.

Men lost already! Sir Leslie, for fear tomorrow's casualty list might rouse the commander in chief's anger, decided to play for safety. He telegraphed Lord Roberts for orders.

The next morning the whole force was once again drawn up in battle formation, ready to go into action. The men's nerves had been strung up for a second time, when a staff officer trotted over, to tell them that the battle had again been postponed.

An urgent message reached Lord Roberts from General Rundle that he was held up 'by powerful forces'. Roberts at once ordered another infantry division out from Bloemfontein to join Rundle, and sent off three brigades of cavalry to make a wide sweep in the north of Dewetsdorp and threaten the Boer rear. De Wet had played the game long enough. He slipped off, taking his prisoners with him. The 25,000 British troops were left standing, with no opposing force to battle.

By the beginning of May, the cold of the South African winter began to check the outbreak of enteric fever. Lord Roberts's 50,000 men, now re-equipped, began to move north, to the Vaal River. They would free the gold mines around Johannesburg, and thereafter occupy the enemy capital of Pretoria.

As the less patriotic or embittered among the Boers drifted back to their farms, the Boer armies dwindled. Those who stayed under arms fell back on Pretoria. When the remaining commandos were concentrated there, Presidents Steyn and Kruger, and their more active generals like Botha, De la Rey and De Wet, who had taken over from the veterans, discovered that they now had only 7,000 soldiers on whom they could fully rely.

The Boer government talked of retreating eastwards from Pretoria, and fighting a rearguard action across the railway down to Delagoa Bay. Meanwhile Botha, De la Rey and the other generals had met in the telegraph office in Pretoria, and discussed seriously whether to end the war there in the capital city, in the conventional way, to prevent the surrounding country from being devastated. Smuts got the gold and war supplies out of the capital, and down the Delagoa Bay railway as the government retreated. There was a brief time of confusion – of willingness to compromise and negotiate – which any British politician who genuinely wanted peace might have turned to good purpose.

But Sir Alfred Milner down in Cape Town, the political brain behind the war, intended to crush Boer independence completely, and to make a new beginning. Though he planned to treat the Boers generously, they must first submit. He insisted as always, on unconditional surrender.

On the Boer side, too, there emerged a political figure who showed the force of character that endures to the end. The Orange Free State had come into this war simply to honour its alliance with the Transvaal. But now President Marcus Steyn of the Orange Free State, a man broken in health but a personality of great force and nobility, declared himself unalterably opposed to peace, if peace might mean the British could begin hanging 'rebels'. Even if the Transvaal signed such a peace, he declared, the Orange Free State would fight on. Henceforward, frail, sick President Steyn, travelling across the veld in a Cape cart with De Wet's commando, became the heart and soul of national resistance.

Marcus Steyn was also a man of high political intelligence. He saw clearly not only that the Boers could still fight on, but that such fighting might regain at least some of the freedom they would otherwise lose. President Kruger, now seventy-five years of age, should go down to Delagoa Bay and away by sea to Europe. There he still might manage to gain political support for the Boer cause from the foreigners who once had been so free with their promises of friendship. Meanwhile, President Steyn would stay and fight on.

When Pretoria itself fell, Lord Roberts believed peace was possible. He arranged a conference with the republican leaders at Zwaar Kop for the ninth of June 1900, and on the eighth an armistice was agreed to by both sides.

The little old general actually had his foot in the stirrup to ride to Zwaar Kop, when a bearded messenger rode up – a Boer in full campaigning kit: wallets, saddlebags, drinking cup, holsters, Mauser rifle, with two full bandoliers across his shoulders and one around his waist. He looked like a man who had readied himself for a long campaign.

'Unless,' he said stiffly to Lord Roberts, 'you have some new proposals to negotiate, I am ordered by General Botha to state that our leaders decline to meet you.'

Lord Roberts was tied by the politicians' demand for un-conditional surrender. The republican leaders knew that if they risked the lives of the Boer 'rebels', they would forfeit their own honour. Roberts might wish above all to save his soldiers' lives, but Milner was determined to win the war on his own terms, whatever the cost might be.

The Boer leaders met at Witbank, and laid their plans. The

army was to be split into small units, which could operate independently. Most of the new commanders were young and professionally untrained. James Hertzog, sent to fight in the Orange Free State, had been a judge. De Wet had been a farmer. De la Rey, a jovial giant and an old soldier, was to go with Smuts, another lawyer, into the wild country of the western Transvaal, where years before the trekkers had fought the Matabele. Louis Botha, also a lawyer by profession, the man who had captured Winston Churchill, was to harass the eastern Transvaal, along the mountain edge that led down to Natal. De Wet – taking with him President Steyn, a president on the run from the enemy – De Wet, the quiet, shrewd, foxy-faced farmer, would be everywhere all at once. He would become a legend of ubiquity and invincibility to the baffled and admiring British. There has never been another guerrilla leader like De Wet.

And how would the British deal with this new kind of war?

A man with a cruel mouth under a heavy moustache was in camp after a hard day's riding across the veld. He was writing a letter to two little boys in England. The problem of the Boer guerrilla was on his mind, too, as this letter showed.

Lord Kitchener was impatient. He was soon to replace Lord Roberts as commander-in-chief here in South Africa, which was something. But only if this war finished quickly would he be in time to grab the greatest prize in his profession – the job, already half promised him, of commander-in-chief in India. The Boers, though, were in no hurry to stop the war. Well, then, they must be taught that fighting the British did not pay. As Sir Alfred Milner had recently said, and rightly, this was, strictly speaking, no longer a war but a police action.

To Julian and Billy Grenfell, the sons of Lord Desborough, Lord Kitchener wrote an interesting letter, in his big, bold handwriting. The boys knew him mainly as a large man with a fund of curious stories about far-off places, who had liked to take them fishing.

My dear Julian and Billy,

Many thanks for your letters . . . I read them while our guns were pounding away at the Boers, who were sitting up on some hills, and trying to prevent our advance. However, they soon cleared out, and ran before we could round them up . . . Sooner or later, we are bound to catch them, but they give a lot of trouble. The Boers are not like the Sudanese, who stood up to a fair fight. They are always running away on their little ponies. We make the prisoners we take march on foot, which they do not like at all. There are a good many foreigners among the Boers, but they are easily shot, as they do not slink about like the Boers themselves. We killed a German colonel yesterday. Now I must go back to work, so good-bye . . .

Slinking about . . . not standing up to a fair fight . . . running away on their little ponies . . . Lord Kitchener, anxious though he was to get away, was to have two exasperating years more of it before at last men came to the conference table and found a reasonable formula for peace.

9

Methods of Barbarism

THE old-style war of armies and pitched battles was over. A new and terrible war of professional soldiers pitted against an entire people was about to begin.

When Kitchener took over supreme command from Lord Roberts, he had a grand total of 210,000 men, and more were coming. But half of them were strung out to protect railway bridges and culverts, or to do garrison duty in hostile little Boer towns.

Boers who had taken the oath of neutrality were being shamed back into active service, one by one. British soldiers found themselves surrounded by a web of hostility and mistrust. Any woman or child they saw might be reporting on their movements to an invisible enemy. Any peaceful farmer might have a Mauser hidden in his thatch, and begin fighting them the next day.

The Boer commandos, probably outnumbered about four to one, but sustained by an entire people and striking unexpectedly, were by about June 1900 successfully preventing the British Army from controlling the country it had occupied.

On Kitchener's orders, the British began to scorch the earth of the Boer homeland.

As early as 3 February 1900, before Lord Roberts gave up his command, Presidents Kruger and Steyn were obliged to protest to him that 'British troops, contrary to the usual usage of war, are guilty of destruction by burning or blowing up with dynamite of farmhouses . . . whereby unprotected women and children are often deprived of food and cover.'

To this, Lord Roberts replied, on 5 February, 'All wanton destruction or injury to peaceful inhabitants is contrary to British practice and tradition, and will if necessary be rigorously repressed by me.' He went on to express his hope that the war would be conducted with 'as little injury as possible to peaceable inhabitants and to private property'. But Lord Roberts had now gone home, and Lord Kitchener was in his place.

It was so easy, a matter of a few moments, to blow a farm-house sky-high with dynamite. Tomorrow only a heap of fragments remained – and the bitterness in the heart of the man who had built it with his own hands.

And what, when their home had been blown up, was to be done with the women and children?

The government in London, advised by Sir Alfred Milner, had willed that the end be unconditional surrender. Against the hostility and resistance of a whole people, only one form of warfare occurred to Kitchener's logical mind. Every farmhouse that might shelter persons who aided the enemy must be destroyed. All livestock must be killed, to deprive the Boer soldiers of food. The Boer soldiers themselves should be treated as wild animals. Let the entire countryside, at whatever expense, be divided into enclosures with barbed wire, so that the elusive horsemen could be trapped as if they were big game.

Once caught, the Boers were to be shipped abroad, to some far-off island like Ceylon or St Helena, so there was no chance of their coming back to fight another day. 'Like wild animals,' said Kitchener, 'they have to go into enclosures before they can be captured.' He talked importantly of his 'weekly bag'.

Instead of farmhouses, he built fortified blockhouses, garrisoned by British soldiers. By the time his scorched-earth system was complete, Kitchener had built and garrisoned eight thousand blockhouses, and laid down barbed wire fences extending for 3,700 miles.

The Boers, however, were not animals but intelligent human beings, most of them deeply religious, of pioneering stock, fighting not for abstract patriotism but for the farms and families which alien enemy soldiers were actually destroying under their very eyes. Since they were in fact men, and not animals, the resistance of the Boers – their will to fight – was never broken by Kitchener's systematic and unimaginative brutality, but rather, it was intensified. Even if the fighting men themselves had wished to give in, their womenfolk, remembering how their homes had been destroyed under their children's eyes, would have shamed them back to the struggle.

While Kitchener's massive reinforcements were still arriving – the army of 80,000 mounted infantry and 160,000 other troops, which from May 1901 onwards were to make all South Africa an armed camp – the small Boer Commandos were able to score some notable successes.

On one occasion, Jacobus De la Rey actually captured Lord Methuen and a thousand of his men, at Tweebosch. The nervous shock to Lord Kitchener was so great that he took to his bed for thirty-six hours, and had to be coaxed with titbits of food by his aide-de-camp. Christiaan De Wet conducted his guerrilla war with the sublime impudence which won him life-long admiration from British soldiers themselves.

One De Wet trick will show his style. Up and down the gaps between his long wire fences, Kitchener sent out mobile columns on patrol, to 'sweep' the countryside and come back with a 'bag' of prisoners. These were the days before radio. Mounted columns on the veld who could not actually see each other found it awkward to communicate. Men hearing rifle fire in the distance were not always able to judge exactly what it signified. The one effective system of signalling in this land of bright sunlight was the heliograph, a hinged mirror which could wink messages.

The commander of one column sent off to chase De Wet

heard distant rifle fire. There were other British columns up ahead, which might perhaps have De Wet cornered. A heliograph began to blink a perfectly correct British message, signed by the officer just out of sight. De Wet was indeed with his back to the wall. If reinforced by one more column, the British could be sure of capturing him.

The British officer set his men at a gallop across the veld towards that heliograph, anxious to arrive in time for the kill. He ran smack into a Boer ambush.

That heliograph message had been sent by De Wet himself.

When a farmhouse was blown up, where should the women and children go?

The name invented for the place where these homeless innocents were sent, a name which first became prominent in South Africa, is one which now prompts a shudder of horror.

Concentration Camps.

Yet these concentration camps in South Africa were not set up, nor were they run, as places of deliberate torture. British soldiers, when in camp, lived in bell tents. The concentration camps, to Kitchener's mind, were merely villages where the houses happened to be bell tents. Boer women and children slept under British army blankets; they ate rations similar to those of the British soldier.

But in South Africa, even the British soldier was badly supplied with rations, not only because of the usual wartime muddle, but also because army stores had such a very long way to come, up a vulnerable railway. If the concentration camps were short of bare necessities, it must often have been because necessities were hard to procure.

Worst, though, were the vast numbers. The officers running the camps were not men hand-picked for their cruelty. They were tied strictly by orders, which forced them to keep these women and children prisoner inside the camp perimeter. They were handicapped by desperate shortages of supply. But, once Kitchener's system got going, it was the numbers that crushed them – truckload after truckload of homeless women and children coming through the gates, until 117,000 were crowded into 47 camps, where they started to die off like flies.

Two days after Christmas, in 1900, a frail-looking English lady of forty, dressed in respectable black, landed at Cape Town, having travelled out from England second class, at her own expense. She had collected £300 from people in England who sympathized with the suffering of the Boers, and she carried a letter of recommendation to Sir Alfred Milner, British High Commissioner.

Emily Hobhouse was the daughter of a village parson in Cornwall. Until five years earlier, when her father died, she had stayed at home, looking after the house, and helping the poor of the parish. After the death of her father, she had much surprised everyone by going off as a missionary to iron miners in the United States, some of whom were Cornish.

In Virginia, Minnesota, she distressed many of the more conventionally minded church folk there by refusing to discriminate, when doing good, among people of different races and religions. When the mines closed down, her work there ended. Returning at last to England, Emily Hobhouse heard of the hardships the South African women were undergoing. She helped organize the South African Women and Children Distress Fund, as a charity, and here she was, in South Africa, with the money. On her voyage out she had begun to master Afrikaans, the language spoken by the Boers.

Sir Alfred Milner granted her an interview – after all, she was well connected, the niece of Lord Hobhouse, an important figure in the Liberal Party. Emily Hobhouse must have seemed to him merely another do-gooder, a maiden lady wishing to practise Christian charity. Sir Alfred confided to Miss Hobhouse that he, personally, thought farm burning 'a mistake'. He spoke cheerfully of the hunt his aide-de-camp had organized for him, to distract his mind from the more dismal side of the war. (They hunted jackals around Table Mountain.) He readily gave her permission to take a carriage full of clothes and food into the Boer republics, though made it clear that, once arrived, what she might do further would depend solely on Lord Kitchener.

One phrase Emily Hobhouse used, when she spoke of farm burning, stuck in Milner's mind. 'How are you going to govern thousands of Joans of Arc?' The maiden lady in black with her charitable impulses and aristocratic connections, was to prove a most formidable opponent of terror in this war.

As Emily Hobhouse rolled north, sleeping on the floor of her carriage, she began to see the first grim evidence of the scorched earth policy. Grassland was strewn with white bones from slaughtered flocks. Farmhouses were blackened heaps of rubble. She also overheard the soldiers talking. Most British regular soldiers disliked destroying farms, and considered turning women and children out of their homes to be unmanly work. There were dozens, however, among the rough-and-ready volunteers, brought together from the ends of the earth, who were evidently beginning to develop a taste for destruction, and to revel in it. Emily Hobhouse, living in the corner of her carriage on bread and jam and cocoa, so as to save every penny for relief supplies, heard such sulphurous talk as gave her a whiff of what to expect in the concentration camps.

Kitchener would not allow her to go further north than Bloemfontein. This did not necessarily mean he wished to prevent her knowing about the camps over the northern horizon. He was only vaguely aware that his camps might be places of horror. He did not once in the entire war make a visit of inspection to a concentration camp.

What Emily Hobhouse saw even around Bloemfontein was bad enough.

She was given a pass allowing her to visit all the women's camps in the locality. The officer in charge of all the camps for the Orange Free State told her, in blunt despair, that he had no transport, no money, and no power to improve the lot of the prisoners. He was not a bad man. Almost none of the camp commandants were. Some laboured long and hard to do what little could be done for their tens of thousands of prisoners. They were simply obeying orders. The man who gave those orders had no imagination, and never went to see what destruction and hardship they caused.

Until Kitchener's scorched-earth policy was applied in South Africa, wars among 'white men' had for many years been wars of soldiers against soldiers. Lord Roberts' boast that the British did not make war on civilians could be made with legitimate pride. The twentieth century was ushered in by the first in a series of brutal wars against whole peoples, wars in which women and children were the victims, sometimes indeed the deliberate victims.

The first camp Emily Hobhouse visited was two miles out of Bloemfontein, on the south slope of a kopje. No trees, no shade – a village of bell tents where two thousand human beings, including nine hundred children, lived under armed guard. All were sleeping on the ground, under army blankets. Since the camp's water supply came from the filthy Modder River, typhoid was striking them down one by one.

Emily Hobhouse had fought typhoid in Minnesota. *Boil all water*, she ordered. There was no fuel. *Keep everything clean.* There was no soap. For babies and nursing mothers, there was no milk. Except for bell tents and blankets, there was nothing. And soon more women and children were expected to arrive, and more, and more, and more, as the depopulation of the veld proceeded.

In the journal Emily Hobhouse kept and the letters she wrote weekly to her aunt, Lady Hobhouse – documents which later caused a political crisis in England – all the grim facts are simply set down, one by one as well as the simple, practical responses which this maiden lady with demonic energy and cold courage made to meet the situation, in face of the unimaginative clumsiness of martial law.

Each tent was provided with a crock to hold water. She had bullied the government into spending £50 to buy crocks. She got an old locomotive boiler to boil the drinking water. She found soap. She collected skinny cows which had escaped the great slaughter of the herds, collected fodder for them, boiled the four bucketfuls of milk they gave each day, and shared it among the babies.

The shortage of clothes was heartbreaking. Shoes and socks had worn away. Women wore dresses made of sacking. When the soldiers burned the farms, they had burned everything – baby clothing, bedding, clothes, flour, seed corn, tools – everything.

Physically the camps were bad, but far worse, Emily Hobhouse found, was the moral atmosphere, a denial of any Christian or other moral principle. This kind of war, against an entire people, meant a final end to manly chivalry. It gave an encouragement to lying, cringing, deception and callousness. Yet she found that none of their hardships, not even seeing their hungry children die before their eyes, would shake the Boer women's determination. They 'never express', wrote Emily Hobhouse, 'a wish that their men must give way. It must be fought out now, they think, to the bitter end.'

Camps varied. Sometimes the commandant had managed to wangle mattresses, and a pure water supply, and even provide some rudimentary medical services. In some, the children were being taught their letters. Some camps were desperate and disease ridden almost beyond belief, camps where the commandant had been unable to cope with the size of his problem; and the women themselves, overwhelmed by misery, and not used to living in such close quarters, a dozen crowded into one tent, had ceased to make any effort towards cleanliness. The most terrifying problem was the death rate. It was later calculated that the mortality among children in the concentration camps, and this figure averages the well-conducted camps with the bad ones, was fourteen times as high as in a British industrial city of that time. Death on this scale had not been known since the days of the Great Plague.

Even before Emily Hobhouse herself returned to England, at the end of May 1901, her horrified uncle, Lord Hobhouse, had shown her letters to Brodrick, the Secretary of State for War. Brodrick, an experienced politician, knew that whether Lord Kitchener liked it or not, something radical must be done at once.

So, while trying hard to send more and better supplies to the camps, Brodrick sent out a commission so chosen that, without falsifying the facts of the concentration camps, its Report would show them publicly in the best possible light. Meanwhile he would play for time, and hope for improvement. But the facts to be found in what became popularly known as the Whitewash Report are themselves appalling.

To begin with, the average death rate among children was 629 per thousand per annum in the Orange Free State, and 585 per thousand per annum in the Transvaal. The rate, of course, in the worst camps, was higher than this. After Emily Hobhouse had spurred the British Government into making elementary improvements, this average death rate fell from 344 in October 1901, to 32 per thousand by April 1902. The British High Command, that is to say, were not being wantonly cruel. They had simply failed to understand the human consequences of what they were doing.

From June to August 1901, alone, during which time the number of people in the camps increased from 85,000 to 105,000, there were 4,067 deaths, of which 3,245 were children.

The Boers themselves estimated, later, that in the course of the war about 26,000 such women and children had died.

Meanwhile, in Britain, as these facts became known, the protests began to spread, from those Liberals like the future Prime Minister, Lloyd George, who had been sympathetic to the Boer cause all along, to others who, having begun by supporting an imperialist policy, were now horrified at its results.

Extracts from Emily Hobhouse's letters were circulated to all members of Parliament, and reprinted in the newspapers. Against his will, Kitchener was at last forced to increase camp rations. Those figures showing an enormous fall in the death rate, therefore, represent actual human lives saved because Miss Hobhouse had the courage to go and see for herself, and thereafter to speak the truth, without being silenced. There were plenty who would have liked to silence her.

Lloyd George, in Parliament, moved the adjournment of the House, to discuss the concentration camps and Miss Hobhouse's report. Sir Henry Campbell-Bannerman, leader of the Liberal Party and another future Prime Minister, coined the phrase which echoed across Britain, when he condemned the waging of the war in South Africa by the 'Methods of Barbarism'.

But how a war against a whole people can be waged, other than by 'Methods of Barbarism', no one had ever shown. The politicians did not want dead children. They wanted unconditional surrender. They could not achieve the one without the other. The soldiers, cruel or humane, callous or chivalrous, were only their obedient instruments.

In the end it was Milner himself, fearing the political consequences of this scandal, who improved the camps. He took them out of the hands of the military, broke up the bigger camps, and got the death rate down to twenty per thousand. He also started educating the children, though, with a certain cynicism, he made sure they could all be taught a view of the war sympathetic to the British Empire.

10

Carry the War to the Enemy!

EARLY in 1901, though they still had about 40,000 armed men they could call on, the shrewdest leaders among the Boers – men of the younger generation, like Botha, Hertzog and Jan Smuts – began to sense that the balance in the war at last had tipped against them.

Kitchener's policy of thorough, deliberate repression was making the veld a hard place to fight over. The territory of the two Boer republics was littered with the shells of burned-out farmhouses, and the rotting corpses of cattle. The aasvogels, South Africa's carrion birds, had multiplied exceedingly since this war began.

Kitchener was beginning to recruit, from waverers or downright traitors among the Boers, a force called the National Scouts, many of whom were familiar with the secrets of the fighting commandos. Waverers like these were going over because the British had begun at last to look like the winning side. Meanwhile the stauncher Boer patriots, when captured, were being shipped to prison camps in countries overseas.

Kitchener approached the British Government that year with a recipe not only for winning the war, but also for solving the crisis of hostility and hatred that everyone knew was bound to come afterwards. He suggested nothing less than the forcible and permanent banishment from South Africa of all Boers who had ever borne arms against the British.

'We have now got more than half the Boer population', he wrote, 'as prisoners of war, or in refugee camps. I think we should start a scheme for settling them elsewhere, and South Africa will then be safe, and there will be room for the

British to colonise.' But, if the entire enemy population could not conveniently be shipped abroad, the trick might be to divide and rule, 'have them hate each other', in Kitchener' words, 'more than they hate the British,' as the patriotic Boers were beginning to hate the National Scouts. However, as the British Cabinet suavely replied, opposing his suggestion, 'Hitherto the effects of severity have not been all that we could have wished.'

Kitchener's personal exasperation expressed itself, as time went on, in further demands for the right to shoot all 'rebels' out of hand, and confiscate their property; or to ship Boer women overseas too, if they proved 'irreconcilable', that is, unwilling to side with the British. But Kitchener could no longer get everything he asked for. Since Emily Hobhouse told of what she saw, the politicians had taken alarm.

On 28 February 1901, General Botha came to Middelburg, on the railway to Delagoa Bay, for a conference with Kitchener and Milner. Big, shrewd Louis Botha was intrigued to find the grim soldier, Lord Kitchener, apparently more anxious than the smooth political representative, Sir Arthur Milner, to reach an agreement that might end the fighting.

Milner's view continued to be that all this fighting was no longer war, but had become a 'police action'. The Boer commandos were not so much soldiers, as armed bandits. Some among them – Boers who originally came, like Jan Smuts, from Cape Colony – Milner considered to be rebels, whom the British had a legal right to hang. His term remained, said Milner, unconditional surrender. The Boers must rely on British generosity to get back, by degrees, some of the rights they had forfeited in making war.

However, Milner hinted, if the Boers did ever get Home Rule in a self-governing British colony, and they might, he was prepared to concede that the system of election should be 'so limited as to ensure the just predominance of the white race'. In other words, Milner held out this bait. The Africans in the Transvaal and the Orange Free State might never be allowed to outvote the white men there, if only the Boers would now submit.

Botha still had one condition to make, and one only. The Boer leaders were prepared to concede that they had lost their independence. They wanted, however, as a term in the peace treaty, an amnesty for those Boers from the Cape and Natal who had taken up arms by the side of their kin, even though technically they might be 'rebels'. This, to Kitcheners' chagrin, Milner refused to concede. Unconditional surrender meant exactly what it said. The rebels must take their chance.

In private, Kitchener pleaded with Milner for the amnesty, remarking that this was 'obviously a point of honour for the Boers'. To the Secretary of State for War he wrote, 'Milner's views may be strictly just, but, to my mind, they are vindictive ... We are now carrying on the war to put two or three hundred Dutchmen in prison at the end of it. It seems to me absurd.'

But Milner wouldn't budge. Botha went back, disappointed, to his companions, and the 'absurd' war continued.

On 20 June 1901 – midwinter in South Africa – the Boer leaders met at Waterval, near Standerton. By now, even the generals were ragged and hungry. Hertzog's command was reduced to twenty men. The great De Wet was hiding in the hills, with a handful of followers. The spirit of the farmers, on whom the fighting men in the field depended, had begun at last to ebb.

The conference was dominated by the two young lawyers, Botha and Smuts. Only one tactic, they urged, could wear down the British will to fight. This war must be carried to the enemy, into the prosperous farmlands of Cape Colony and Natal, where men of Boer stock would sustain their fighting men from farms the British might think twice before they burned. The place to fight the British was not here, in the devastated territory of the high veld, but on their very doorstep.

This was a policy which had been tried more than once, unsuccessfully. But what other hope was there? They must try again.

Jan Smuts, himself the son of a Cape farmer, was just thirty-one. The way he dressed on commando still bore a touch of the Cambridge-educated lawyer – it showed in his collar and sober cravat, in the felt hat he wore flat-brimmed instead of slouched, in the coloured handkerchief neat in his breast pocket. He rode a chestnut gelding called Charlie. Except for the pistol in his brass-buckled belt, Jan Smuts might have been a country attorney, riding in from his farm to the courthouse. He carried books in his saddlebag and, by the light of the campfire, would read himself to sleep with the Greek Testament, or Xenophon's *Anabasis*, or Kant's *Critique of Pure Reason*. There was a similar combination of a farmer's instinct for country, and a lawyer's cold logic about the way he fought.

Throughout July, Smuts carefully prepared the raid, which was to distress the British and save the lives of the 'rebels'.

Smuts took 362 hand-picked men, devoted to the national cause, who were veterans in war. By the time his job was done, half of them were to be dead. His right-hand man was Field Cornet Jacobus van Deventer, a tall, heavy, moustached man, with intense narrow eyes, utterly loyal, the only comrade-in-arms with whom Smuts would willingly discuss his plans.

Smuts began by dividing his command into two. This might make it easier to cut through British wire, and slip past enemy patrols. The rendezvous with van Deventer was at Zastron, a village just north of the Orange River, and twenty miles from the mountainous border of neutral Basutoland.

Inspecting his command at the start, Smuts felt like the

leader not of soldiers but of beggars on horseback. His men wore clothes made of gunny sacks, and home-made sandals held together by thongs of rawhide. Ammunition was low; some had no more than one clip of ammunition for their Mauser rifles. Shirts and undershirts had long ago worn out. Horses were in fair condition, because after the winter rains the grass was growing again on the veld, and even Lord Kitchener could not stop the grass from growing.

That first morning spirits were high. The Boers were cooking their rations, of biltong, or dried meat, and filling their water bottles, when, through the morning mist, enemy soldiers opened fire. An Australian column had tracked them down before their raid was even begun.

'Those are the Australians we've beaten once before, at Zwartruggens,' said Smuts calmly. 'They've come back for more.'

The Boers, obeying his whispered orders, faded into the veld. Before the sun was halfway up the drab morning sky, the Australians were surrounded and defeated. Smuts' men moved back to camp, driving a bunch of Australian prisoners before them.

'Undress,' said Smuts.

Off came the Australian boots and trousers. The tall, lean Australians stood there in their fluttering khaki shirt-tails, bare-foot. 'Now march,' said Smuts. 'We're not taking prisoners today.'

From now onward, the plan in Smuts' command would be to clothe, arm and feed his men off the enemy.

The long ride south across the Orange Free State was a nightmare, and not only because of British wire and British patrols, though at one time nine columns were trying to close in on Smuts. Nor did they let the continuous pouring rain and violent electric storms deter them. What hardened their hearts was to see the fertile countryside changed to a desert.

Each night, by the fire, Smuts made notes in his diary. On

the twenty-fifth of July, near Edenburg, he notes, 'Found myself surrounded on all sides, and driven on railway line. Had to flee from sun-up to sunset.' Next day, he writes, 'Enemy still in pursuit . . . My position is precarious; horses much done up; burghers dispirited. Still, I shall press on till end.'

The British had already got word that Smuts was trying to break out of the country. Kitchener sent orders to General French, commanding his cavalry, to hold all possible crossings of the Orange River, and block the way south. He sent off four large mounted columns, to stick close to Smuts' heels.

There were enemy tents and troops everywhere. Smuts and his men covered the country like ghosts, moving at night or during storms, cutting enemy wire under cover of darkness. The Boers had not the cumbersome equipment of the British mounted infantry – they travelled light – but the journey south was a bad dream of miserable wet and cold, saddening devastation, and constant danger. Sometimes tough veterans tumbled from the saddle with weariness and hunger, or died on the march from exposure.

They reached Zastron at last. The Orange River, ahead of them, swollen by winter rains, had still to be crossed. Reliable van Deventer made the rendezvous, with his detachment of men, but reported that the British now had put a price of five thousand dollars on Jan Smuts' head, dead or alive. Kitchener had also issued a new order that all Boers wearing khaki were to be shot. The Boers now using Australian breeches had no intention, however, of going back to wearing old sacks. If, like Smuts himself, they came from the Cape, they were liable to be shot or hanged, anyway. Kitchener's policy of 'severity' was beginning to wear itself out.

A follower of Smuts called Louis Wessels came from this odd corner of the Orange Free State, which bordered on the neutral native state of Basutoland, safe amid its high mountains. All known crossings of the river were heavily guarded by the British, but Louis Wessels spoke of a narrow gorge, up in the mountains, near where the great Orange River rose from its source, where none would expect horsemen to cross.

'And is a crossing there on horseback possible?' asked Smuts, with a lawyer's logic.

Louis Wessels avoided his eyes. 'Just barely possible,' he muttered.

The trail into mountainous Basutoland was hard on men and ponies. The precipitous path down into that gorge was a giddy horror. Horses lost their footing; men fell tumbling to their death. But, by 4 September, over a month since their march began, Smuts' men had swum their horses across the dark, swirling Orange River, and stood on British soil in Cape Colony.

When Smuts that morning called the roll, he found that of the 362 men who set out with him, only 250 remained – 250 Boers who, having seen the devastated farms of the high veld, would die in their boots rather than surrender.

Southwards, the country was open plain, with little cover. Jan Smuts wheeled about, and headed for the protection of the high land. Some stragglers, mounted on worn-out horses, were attacked by three hundred superbly mounted Basutos, who, neutral though they were, sympathized with the British, and, like all natives in South Africa, hated the Boers. Thirty horses were lost, and six men died. Smuts, riding back too late to help in the skirmish, found that those of the dead men who had fallen into the hands of the Basutos were hideously mutilated.

Mountainous country was safer than open grassland. Smuts' plan was to cross the high plains of South Africa by moving from one mountain range to another south and west, as if going down the rungs of a ladder. The winter rains had set in, and Smuts' men rode southwards in threadbare clothes which never dried.

7 September found them fifty miles south of the Orange River, near Dordrecht, in the raw and misty Stormberg

Mountains. The only way out was through a narrow defile called Moordenaars Poort. Jan Smuts knew there were British troops on the far side of the mountain. He always had better information than the enemy because, even though this was their own colony, the British were operating in hostile territory. Almost every farmhouse in the Stormberg Mountains was a Boer farmhouse, willing to help with information, and perhaps with food, clothes and horses. This was the country from which many of the original trekkers had come. But now, if the British had blocked Moordenaars Poort, Smuts' commando would be trapped.

The three scouts whom Smuts sent into Moordenaars Poort, Japie Neethling and the two brothers Adendorff, said the pass itself was clear, though the British had encamped beyond. Jan Smuts was never one to underestimate his enemy. He knew the British soldier had copied many Boer tricks in the past two years, and, like all Boer generals, he was willing to reconnoitre the ground in person. At four in the afternoon, Jan Smuts and his scouts rode a second time into the ambush defile.

'If we're ambushed,' warned Jan Smuts, 'it's every man for himself.' The scouts said nothing. If the commandant, not trusting their opinion, wanted to make sure and double sure, that was his own business.

As they rode towards Moordenaars Poort there were no signs of life. The defile was temptingly open – a clear way out of the wet, cold mountains to the fertile plain beyond.

The British, however, had learned the art of ambush. They opened fire on the four Boer horsemen from one shoulder of the defile, at a range of only twenty yards. Their first volley killed one of the Adendorff brothers, and badly wounded both the other Adendorff and Japie Neething. Smuts' faithful chestnut, Charlie, was shot from under him. Smuts kicked his feet clear from the stirrups, and was amazed to find himself on the ground, unhurt. He sprinted down the defile, racing for his life.

The British had come out of ambush, now, and like

sportsmen taking potshots were firing excitedly at the slight, fair-haired figure which dodged from thorn bush to boulder. Suddenly, Smuts disappeared.

He had found a donga at his feet – a deep ravine, washed out of the mountain soil by flash floods. He jumped straight down into it, out of sight. By the time the khaki-clad British, rifles in hands came thudding in their heavy boots to the lip of the donga, Smuts was gone.

Captain Hughes, the British officer commanding the ambush party, confidently reported that Smuts had been wounded. It was a miracle that he had escaped unscathed. Smuts arrived back at the Boer camp at Allenspoort late at night, footsore from his long walk, but otherwise without a scratch.

The two wounded Boers were taken by the British to a nearby farm, where Mrs Shoenmann, a Boer woman, lived. Before they died of their wounds, they whispered to her in Afrikaans to go where the pony Charlie had been shot and rescue the commandant's saddlebags, which the British had foolishly overlooked. Mrs Shoenmann got the bags and buried them, so that, after the war, Jan Smuts got back not only his diary and notes, but his well-thumbed copies of the Greek Testament, Xenophon and Kant.

An interesting fact was that the British, officers and men alike, often disobediently blunted the sharp edge of Kitchener's more brutal orders. All through the war, for instance, Boers continued to send their wounded to British field dressing stations, where they were as carefully looked after as the British soldiers who the day before might have been hunting them down. The policy of scorched earth and concentration camp – war waged against women and children – disgusted the best among the British, just as it stiffened the resolve of the best among the Boers.

Since there was evidently no way out through Moordenaars Poort, Jan Smuts's commando was bottled up in the inhospitable Stormberg Mountains, and the British knew it. They moved in to finish him off.

The commando was dwindling not only in numbers, but in its power of movement. The tough Boer ponies, which could be pushed to do sixty miles a day, were suffering from cold even worse than their hard-bitten masters. In one night at Allenspoort, thirty horses died from exposure.

Smuts had started a new diary, and it tells, in brief phrases, of this temporary retreat, as the British moved in to corner Smuts, and finish him: 'Sept. 10th, Allenspoort: Enemy repulsed; eleven forces move to surround me. Sept. 11th: Marched by Gardiner's bridle path through English forces half an hour apart.' The entry for 12 September continues: 'Towards afternoon enemy forces overtook me, and an action took place on Stapelberg. Enemy losses 50 or 60.'

The weary, hungry Boer horsemen stood at bay on a high plateau. All around, in the darkness, were the British. The columns under Colonel Munro had skilfully converged. Once daylight came, Colonel Munro knew he could force Smuts' surrender, at leisure.

The Boers knew they were in a trap, which the rising of the sun would spring. The 'rebels' among them, including the commandant himself, had perhaps nothing better to look forward to than a firing squad. The rest would be shipped to imprisonment overseas.

Towards them, out of the thick mist and the dark of night, came the odd thud of someone limping on a crutch.

'If you stay here,' said the cripple, simply, in Afrikaans, 'the British will catch you.'

'Is there a way down from this plateau?' asked Smuts. His scouts had not found one.

'You can go down the way I climbed up.'

One or two of the weary, disconsolate men smiled. A path that a hunchback with a crutch had climbed must be easy for horsemen.

'No British?'

'Not the way I shall take you.'

But before dawn broke, there were some of Smuts's commando who almost wished they had taken their chances of surrender to the British. This hunchback began to seem less of an angel in disguise than a demon from the underworld. Despite his crutch, he could slither and scramble down mountain declivities where a grown man leading a horse dare hardly glance without a shudder. But they all got down.

In the morning, Colonel Munro's troops advanced on the plateau, to find Jan Smuts miraculously gone.

No commando had ever penetrated this far into Cape Colony. Smuts heard that Louis Botha was at the same time raising a similar havoc in Natal. The new strategy was proving itself. But the more his successes raised the hearts of the Cape Colony Boers, the more important it became for the British to catch Jan Smuts. Newly arrived mounted infantry were used extravagantly to block the way of Smuts's handful of ragged horsemen, and run him down. In the end, his one small commando was occupying the attention of 35,000 British soldiers!

After breaking out of the Stormberg, Smuts's men began ambushing trains. They almost captured General French himself. But they were obliged to move on, making a forced march through icy, driving rain, with the British after them. They were in the saddle continuously for sixty hours. For all of them 15 September 1901 was the worst night of the war. Their clothes were solid boards of ice on their backs, though the icy mud through which the ponies plodded never quite froze. Twelve men dropped from exhaustion that night and died in the cold; sixty horses died. It took the men who survived six hours to cover three miles.

On 17 September the British made contact with them again. They had not, after all, escaped pursuit. They were being harried by two mounted columns, under Colonel Gorringe and Colonel Doran. This was the lowest, bleakest point of the raid. Food, ammunition, horses, and strength were nearly all gone. It was a moment when a lesser man than Jan Smuts would have given up.

Scouts came back to report that in camp ahead of them

were the 17th Lancers, a crack British cavalry regiment. Smuts drew his men around him. 'In that camp,' he told them soberly, 'is all that we need – food, horses, ammunition, warm clothing.'

'Tea?' asked a joker.

'Tea. We must supply ourselves from our enemy. To-night, we attack.'

Such sublime audacity was more than the British cavalry-men were prepared for. The attackers had the irresistible desperation of men who have suffered and hungered. There were not only tea and food in that camp, but also warm uniforms, and well-groomed cavalry chargers. Smuts' men also captured an Armstrong gun, and a Maxim. The com-mando was one step closer to being an army.

By 5 October they were equipped to fight a miniature battle. The British column under Colonel Gorringe was press-ing them close. The Boers turned, as if brought to bay, but they had chosen their ground well. The British attacked impulsively, into the crossfire of the newly munitioned riflemen, and the heavy weapons they had captured. The British lost nine hundred horses, and left two hundred men dead on the field.

Smuts at once split his force into two parties. He again gave command of the second party to van Deventer, the man he trusted. 'We will rendezvous this time,' he ordered, 'by the sea.'

The horsemen led by Smuts himself reached the seacoast west of the Cape of Good Hope in December 1901. Most of the men had never seen the sea before. They rode their horses into the creaming waves, exulting like school-boys. The unit looked in good shape. Since the terrible night of the frozen rains, it had grown in numbers. Volunteers were coming in from little Boer towns, where Smuts' now legendary exploits were inspiring a new resistance. Still another ambush on the British had been successful, and the horsemen were loaded down with military supplies.

Smuts set up headquarters at van Rhynsdoorp, in the

valley of the Doorn River, close to his own home. He had enough men now to form three separate commandos, and he pushed his mounted patrols to within sight of Cape Town itself.

These were not the naked, scorched cattle farms of the veld, but country rich in fruit and corn. His men fared well. Little townships of thatched white houses crowded around a church to form a square. At night the Afrikaans-speaking farmers, to whom the whole war so far had been hearsay, came to whisper the latest exploit of Jan Smuts, or to recount how this bold young man or the other had ridden off to join him.

Martial law was being enforced right through Cape Colony, and even in the ports. The strategy of invading the Cape had succeeded. Tens of thousands of British troops were kept busy, hunting for elusive Boer commandos which rode everywhere, and struck where they chose, yet even now amounted in all to only four thousand men.

The brave and dogged Boer resistance had begun to win the tough farmers new friends overseas. Not only were their supporters in Britain itself gaining in political influence, but the present British Government was being held up to international contempt. Every new repression and cruelty employed against the Boers isolated Britain further from the comity of nations.

In January 1902 young Queen Wilhelmina of the Netherlands offered to mediate between the Boers, most of whom were of Dutch origin, and their British enemies. Still hoping for an outright victory, the British declined. But it was a sign of the times.

Smuts, using homemade dynamite hand grenades, had made a successful attack on the copper-mining town of O'Okiep. He had bottled up Colonel Sheldon there, and was organizing a blockade to starve him out when he saw a Cape cart approach, under the sign of the white flag.

Smuts expected this to indicate the surrender of the town he was besieging. But the Cape cart bore two officers, with a personal letter to himself from Lord Kitchener. Boers and British were meeting at Vereeniging to discuss peace; General Smuts's presence was requested. Smuts was given a safe conduct, and was escorted to British-occupied Port Nolloth with military honours.

I I

Peace at Last

LORD Kitchener of Khartoum, expert at dictating terms to
conquered Orientals, knew when to use pomp in order to
impress.

When he met Jan Smuts at Kroonstad, Lord Kitchener
was mounted on a magnificent black charger, amid an
escort of Pathan cavalry, picturesque in turbans. His manner, when he sat opposite Smuts in the privacy of the railway carriage, was affable, even friendly. He pointed out
that 400,000 British troops were now opposing a mere 18,000
Boers. If the Boers were to surrender, the British would be
magnanimous.

Jan Smuts did not say much, but thought a great
deal.

The mind of this Cambridge-educated lawyer, who now,
at thirty-two, was Assistant Commandant General of the
Boer forces in the field, could work lightning-fast. What
reasons lay behind this peace conference at Vereeniging?
Sixty Boer leaders, including Presidents Steyn and Schalk
Burger (taking Kruger's place) were to meet there, and,
with Kitchener's consent, begin by discussing whether to
surrender or fight on.

The sight of his old comrades, when he met them at Vereeniging on 15 May, was a terrible shock to Jan Smuts. He knew
at once one good reason why this conference had been
called. The men at the Cape, their hard ride south once
accomplished, had lived off the fat of the land. But these
men whose duty obliged them still to fight across the devastated republics were starving. They were clad in skins and

sacking, and their bodies were covered with sores. They were reaching the limit of human endurance.

Hardships alone, however, had not brought them to the point of surrender. To De Wet, fiery-hearted, unconquerable in spirit, this war was still a 'war of religion', in which 'God was seeking to make a nation worthy of his name'. President Steyn, broken in body but strong of will, said that loss of independence would mean loss of self-respect. Schalk Burger considered it had been a 'war of miscalculation' – the Boers from the first underestimating their enemy. In one way he was right. Big old De la Rey wondered whether, supposing the leaders continued to fight the war, the men in the field would follow them. Calm shrewd Louis Botha spoke quietly with Smuts about the need for a peace to 'save the nation'. But what sort of peace could they achieve? Were the British as overpoweringly strong as Kitchener had asserted?

Jan Smuts watched and reflected, but spoke little, giving himself time to make up his mind.

The cards were by no means all in Kitchener's hands. He had made a desert of the Transvaal and the Orange Free State. But was he now to apply the scorched-earth policy to the Cape of Good Hope as well, simply because Smuts was fighting there with such amazing success? The war had dragged on, and was costly. How much longer might the taxpayer – the voter – foot the bill?

The Boers' foreign friends were beginning to rally, at long last. Again the Dutch tried to mediate. Speaking for his colleagues, Baron Kuyper offered the Netherlands Government as intermediaries. The Liberals, under Campbell-Bannerman and Lloyd George, after denouncing the 'Methods of Barbarism' used in the concentration camps, had gone on to declare publicly that they were in favour of granting the Boers self-government after the war. And in Britain, the Liberals were thought likely to win the next general election.

But there was another fear in the minds of Boer and Briton alike.

The Bantu also had suffered in this war. When the veld was cleared of living creatures, a hundred thousand Africans also – innocent bystanders in this war – had been thrust into British concentration camps. Millions of South African natives had seen the all-powerful British beaten in battle; they had seen the cruel Boers hunted down like wild animals. The Bantu knew they outnumbered the white men occupying their country a dozen to one, and were beginning slowly – and peaceably, as yet – to draw their own conclusions.

Kitchener found Schalk Burger gloomy and silent. Marcus Steyn, though sick, was the dominating personality among the Boers – 'the man who rules the whole' – and a convinced bitter-ender. Both, Kitchener discovered with a sigh of relief, were 'gentlemen'. 'They are much afraid of a native rising,' he reported, 'and I have told them they are entirely responsible if such an event occurs.'

Negotiations went on in the large tented camp the British had prepared at Vereeniging. Starving men from the veld swapped experiences and expressed opinions, and ate good food, and changed their rawhide and sackcloth for clothes. British soldiers, who a few days before had been hunting them down, stood around, treating them with respect, as plenipotentiaries.

Negotiations, the British declared, must be direct with Kitchener himself. They were having no truck with Dutch or any other intermediaries. Sir Alfred Milner, now Lord Milner, and busy putting life into the devastated economy of the Transvaal, was at Kitchener's elbow. Milner, however, was in no mood to make concessions. The Transvaal was beginning to pay. The gold mines on the Rand were working once more. The Stock Exchange had opened in Johannesburg as long ago as last December. Speculation in gold and diamond shares went on as before, while out on the veld the cruel fighting had continued.

The Boer negotiators once more found that the hated and dreaded Kitchener, still secretly anxious to get away to India, was a somewhat easier man to come to terms with than supple, clever Milner.

The Boer leaders had first to decide among themselves whether or not to carry on the long fight.

The Transvaal delegates – and in this lay Milner's last hope of 'divide and rule' – thought the game was up, though tough old De la Rey was not wholly convinced. But Steyn and De Wet, from the Orange Free State – the most brilliant general, and the most dedicated political leader – would have fought on forever. However, rather than allow the British to split one republic from the other, they submitted to a majority vote.

When it came to counting heads, fifty-four were for making a peace – six for fighting on. Smuts himself finally put it this way. 'It's better to negotiate an orderly peace now, under the best possible terms, than to be crushed later, and have ignominious terms thrust upon us.'

An 'orderly peace' would need to be something better than unconditional surrender. Smuts's nimble lawyer's mind was already working out ways to strike the best bargain.

'If we consider this as a military matter,' Smuts told his comrades bluntly, 'then I must admit we can still go on with the struggle . . . But we are not here as an army. We are here as a people. Burghers, we decided to stand to the bitter end. Let us now, like men, admit that the end has come for us, in a more bitter shape than we thought . . . We bow to God's will.'

The sixty Boer leaders at Vereeniging having decided to make peace, appointed five of their number – Botha, De la Rey, De Wet, Hertzog and Smuts – to confer with Kitchener and Milner in Pretoria. Marcus Steyn, a consistent bitter-ender, had resigned his presidency, rather than take part in the negotiations. De la Rey and De Wet were good soldiers, and no more. On Hertzog, Botha and Smuts, three lawyers, the hard bargaining actually depended.

Lord Milner made his position clear from the start – every concession now meant trouble later. Kitchener was more adroit, and ready to give way. Terms were slowly decided upon.

The Boers must lay down their arms, and take an oath of allegiance to King Edward VII. There was no arguing with that. The independence of the republics was over, and the Boers knew it. Those who swore the oath would regain their property. Afrikaans was to go on being used as the language in schools and courts. No war reparations would be exacted from the devastated Boer countryside. Indeed, to get the scorched earth productive again, to raise roof-trees and re-stock farms, the British were prepared to grant a loan of £3 million on easy terms.

British subjects who had aided the Boers – 'rebels' – were to be excluded from the amnesty. Alas, there was no arguing with that one, either. But Smuts, himself technically liable to be sentenced to death, lost all fear, as he watched the negotiations, that he or any other Cape Boer would end with a noose around his throat. That clause was put in to save face, especially Lord Milner's face.

Smuts got the British to yield one concession which Milner later referred to as 'the greatest mistake of my life'. The Boers were being promised representative institutions, eventually, under the British Crown, possibly the type of self-government that the Cape, for example, or Canada and Australia enjoyed. But, when that happened, should the Bantu get the vote? On this one issue, the peace conference might have split. The Boers' attitude to the Africans had always been 'Crush or be crushed'. The British, on the other hand, subtler in their tolerance, had hopes of using the natural majority of coloured voters as a political counterweight against the Boers.

'Why not postpone the issue of granting a coloured vote,' said Jan Smuts, with deceptive helpfulness, 'from the time when representative institutions are granted, to the time when self-government is granted?'

Nobody quite grasped what those words meant. Everyone was glad to postpone a difficult problem for others to solve later. The negotiators shrugged, and accepted.

But would self-governing Boers ever grant the vote to their own Africans? Of course not, though Milner himself saw the point too late, and lived to regret it. Smuts had won the day, because, with that seemingly tiny victory at the negotiating table – that postponed decision – a future Boer predominance in South Africa was assured, and without a shot being fired. The Boers in the long run would outvote the British, and deny the vote to the Africans, who otherwise would have an automatic and immense majority. From Vereeniging onwards, Smuts and the other Boer leaders, in one way or another, set themselves patiently to win back, by political means, the republican independence that had been lost by the gun.

The treaty was signed on 31 May 1902 – without enthusiasm, but without opposition, by the Boer leaders, except for President Steyn, who, with a few loyal companions, followed President Kruger into exile.

Winter was coming on. Could the Boer commandos, De Wet wondered, have fought through yet another winter? His famous white horse and his Mauser rifle were all he now possessed in the world. De Wet sat in the saddle, and began to ponder.

On 17 June the grateful Stock Exchange and the now flourishing gold-mining corporations of the Rand gave a victory banquet in Johannesburg, to honour Lord Kitchener and the other senior commanders of the British Army.

Kitchener had removed from public parks in Bloemfontein and Pretoria all the full-sized statues he could find of such Boer leaders as President Kruger. He had them crated up and shipped to England, to adorn the park of his private house.

But elections in 1906 brought the Liberals to power in Britain, and gave South Africans the democratic constitution they had been promised. Kitchener was obliged to send his collection of statues back to South Africa. Het Volk, the party then most representative of the Boers, won a majority in the Transvaal. President Steyn, their leader in exile, sent instructions to big, genial, good-hearted Louis Botha to become Prime Minister. Botha, who hated the prospect, would have taken that order from no one but Marcus Steyn. Jan Smuts became a minister in Botha's government, and later, first Botha, then Smuts became successively Prime Ministers of the Union of South Africa – the federal state within which British and Boers alike sought to live together, and to heal the scars of war. With the Boers once more a political force, the vexed question of votes for Africans in the Orange Free State and the Transvaal disappeared from the order of the day.

After a war, the butcher presents his bill. Six thousand British were killed in action, and sixteen thousand died of enteric fever. Fourteen thousand Boers died in action. The cost to the British taxpayer was £220 million.

The brunt of the war fell on the women and children. A memorial near Bloemfontein, the South African National Monument, now commemorates the 26,000 women and children who met unnecessary deaths in the war of 1899–1902.

Three people – three heroes – are buried under this monument: two men, General De Wet and President Steyn; and an English lady: Emily Hobhouse.

Further Reading

AFTER a war, the history is usually written by the victors. Most histories, therefore, given account of the Boer War from the British point of view. Only a few biographies and memoirs give insight into the Boer viewpoint, and no book was to be found giving a picture of the war through the eyes of a Bantu.

A complete picture of South Africa, from earliest to modern times, not altogether unsympathetic to the Boers, and even acknowledging the existence of the Bantu, is given in the *Cambridge History of the British Empire, Vol. VIII* (Cambridge University Press, 1936).

A lively account of the fighting from a patriotic British standpoint is given by the 'Sherlock Holmes' man, A. Conan Doyle, in his *Great Boer War* (Smith, Elder, 1900) but it says nothing of the last eighteen months of guerrilla war.

L. C. M. S. Amery's *The Times History of the War in South Africa* (7 vols., Sampson Low, 1900–7) is brisk and thorough.

Sir J. F. Maurice wrote the British official *History of the War in South Africa* (4 vols., 1899–1902). In 1902 Smuts and De la Rey gave materials towards an understanding of the Boer side in their *Official Reports . . . Relating to the War in South Africa* (1902).

Here are some books which give more information about different aspects of this book which may have interested you:

Eric A. Walker's *The Great Trek*, 3rd ed. (A. & C. Black, 1948) is a first-class historical narrative, and M. Juta's *The*

Pace of the Ox (a life of Paul Kruger) (Constable, 1937) is more interesting than Kruger's own laboured *Memoirs* (T. Asher & Unwin, 2 vols., 1902).

S. G. Millin's *Rhodes* (Chatto & Windus, 1952) gives an overly respectful account, and W. Plomer's *Cecil Rhodes* (Peter Davies, 1933) perhaps an overcritical account, of the diamond multimillionaire's legendary career, of which many facts still remain hidden in the shadows.

S. G. Millin also wrote a two-volume *General Smuts* (Faber & Faber, 1936) a semi-official biography; but a less hero-worshipping and more humane tone, interestingly enough, is to be found in Smuts' son's less expert *Jan Christian Smuts* (Cassell, 1952). The best account of Smuts' commando raid into the Cape, and one of the best books about irregular warfare ever written, is D. Reitz, *Commando* (Faber & Faber, 1929). Christiaan De Wet wrote about his own experiences in *Three Years' War* (Archibald, Constable & Co., 1902), but, alas, he was better with a rifle than a pen.

J. van der Poel wrote a good book called *The Jameson Raid* (Oxford, 1952) and there is an earlier, less well-informed account with the same title by H. Marshall Hole (Philip Allen, 1930). The defence of Mafeking is described in *Mafeking* (Cassell, 1968) by Bryan Gardner.

There are two biographies of Kitchener, a rather dull official one, in 3 volumes, by Sir G. Arthur (Macmillan, 1920) and a brilliant one by Sir Philip Magnus, sympathetic, skilfully documented and revealing: *Kitchener: Portrait of an Imperialist* (John Murray, 1958). Emily Hobhouse's *Report* was published in London in 1901, and a friend wrote a memoir of her, after her death, but she, too, is relatively unknown today.

The rivalry between Britain and Germany in South Africa is discussed from an American viewpoint by W. Bixler in *Anglo-German Imperialism in South Africa* (1932). The most objective and professional view of the fighting is in the two volumes of the German General Staff's *The War in South Africa* (1904–6). B-P's nephew, B. F. S. Baden-Powell, wrote an interesting but much more amateur analysis of the military lessons in *The Boer War* (Isbister, 1903).

People involved on both sides wrote about the war, and how it affected them personally, in books still worth reading. J. F. C. Fuller in *Last of the Gentlemen's Wars* (Faber & Faber, 1937) saw the war as a young but intelligent professional soldier; H. W. Nevinson, *Ladysmith* (Methuen, 1900) as a skilled journalist seeing a siege close to; and P. Pienaar, *With Steyn and De Wet* (Methuen, 1902) as a Boer soldier.

Winston Churchill could never write other than from a patriotic British point of view, but about South Africa he had a human sympathy with the Boers, and wrote wonderfully well. The early and rare books reprinted from his newspaper dispatches, in *Frontiers and Wars* (Eyre & Spottiswoode, 1962) have lost by being abridged. A more interesting account of his adventures in South Africa is contained in *Roving Commission: My Early Life* (Thornton & Butterworth, 1930), published when he was less famous, and, therefore, more indiscreet.

Index

Afrikaans, 10, 17, 35, 122, 146

Baden-Powell, Col. Robert, 75–9, 80–86
Bantu, 10, 14, 27, 31, 144, 146
Barnato, Barney, 30
Barr-Campbell, Gen., 113
Basutoland, 28, 133–4
Basutos, 134
Bechuanaland, 32
Beit, Alfred, 35
Black Velvet, 31, 40, 42
Black Week, 53, 57, 58, 62, 73
Blesberg, 21–2
Bloemfontein, 90, 91, 104, 106, 107, 109, 111, 123, 148
Blood River, Battle of, 23
Boer, meaning of, 9; way of life, 14; repression of Africans, 10, 36
Botha, Louis, 66–7, 114, 115, 116, 129–30, 143, 145, 148
Bower, Sir Graham, 42
British, arrive in South Africa, 10; take over from Dutch, 14; ease lot of Africans, 15; and slavery, 23; take over Natal, 23–5; losses in Black Week, 62; react against Kitchener's harshness, 124, 127
Broadwood, Col. R. G., 108–11

Brodrick, William St John Fremantle, 126
Bulawayo, 39
Buller, Gen. Sir Redvers, 58–62, 63, 73
Bushmen, 10
Butler, Sir William, 48

Campbell-Bannerman, Sir Henry, 127, 143
Cape Colony, 90, 129, 134, 138, 140
Cape of Good Hope, 9, 139, 143
Cape Town, 37, 51, 89, 140
Chamberlain, Joseph, 45, 49
Chermside, Sir Herbert, 112
Churchill, Lord Randolph, 38
Churchill, Winston, 63–73, 116
Clery, Sir Francis, 73
Colenso, Battle of, 58–62, 111
Colvile, Gen., 96, 99, 101, 102, 109, 111
Concentration camps, 121–2, 123–7, 136
Coventry, Capt. the Hon. Charles, 39
Creusot gun, 79–80, 83
Cronje, Commandant Piet, 44, 51, 54, 78–80, 89–91, 92–104

'Death Trap', 64–5
De la Rey, Jacobus, 114, 116, 120, 143, 145
Desborough, Lord, 116
Deventer, Field Cornet Jacobus van, 131, 133, 139
De Wet, Christiaan, 91, 95, 102, 109–12, 116, 120–21, 130, 143, 145, 148
Dundonald, Lord, 59
Durban, 51, 54
Dutch East India Co., 9
Dutch Reformed Church, 10, 17

Edward VII, King, 146
Eloff, Commandant, 84, 85
Enteric fever, 107–8, 111, 114

Farrar, Sir George, 41, 43
FitzClarence, Capt., 79
Franchise, for Uitlanders, 48–9; for Africans, 146–7, 148
French, Gen. Sir John, 57, 90–93, 96, 98–9, 101, 133, 138
French Huguenots, 9, 14

Gatacre, Gen Sir W., 57–8
George, Lloyd, 126–7, 143
Germany, Germans, 9, 45, 49, 74
Gorringe, Col., 139
Goshen, 31–2, 33
Great Trek, 11, 13–14, 17–18, 37, 108
Grey, Maj. Sir Raleigh, 39

Hannay, Gen., 97, 99, 100, 101–2

Hertzog, James, 116, 128, 130, 145
Hobhouse, Emily, 122–7, 129, 148
Hobhouse, Lady, 124
Hobhouse, Lord, 122, 126
Hopetown, 27
Hore, Col., 84
Hottentots, 10, 24
Hughes, Capt., 136

Impi, Zulu and Matabele battle formation, 20, 21

Jameson, Dr Leander Starr, 38–45
Jameson Raid, 38–45, 54, 75, 83
Johannesburg, 34, 36, 39, 40, 42, 144, 147
Joubert, Petrus, 34, 51, 53, 54, 59, 66

Kaffirland, 14, 18
Kelly-Kenny, Gen., 92, 96, 99, 100, 102
Kimberley, 28, 29, 39, 54–5
Kitchener, Horatio Herbert, First Earl Kitchener of Khartoum, 74, 87–91, 92–102, 116–20, 123–4, 127, 129–30, 133, 136, 141, 142–5, 147–8
Kruger, Paul, 13–17, 18, 19, 20, 22, 25, 31, 32, 33, 36, 37, 41–6, 47, 49, 50, 53, 105, 147

Ladysmith, 53, 54, 59, 60, 63, 64, 66, 73, 74, 105
Lee-Metford rifle, 49

Lindley, David, 22
Lippert, 37

Mafeking, 39; siege of, 75–86
Magersfontein, Battle of, 55–7, 62, 82, 90, 91
Mahon, Col., 86
Maritz, Gert, 21
Matabele, 16, 18, 20, 22, 38; fighting methods of, 19; beaten by Boers on Great Trek, 19–22
Mauser gun, 49, 53, 59, 61
Maxim gun, 51, 54, 59
Methuen, Lord, 55, 56, 80, 82, 120
Milner, Sir Alfred, 47–50, 89, 105, 114, 119, 122, 123, 127, 129–30, 144–7
Mocke, Jan, 25
Munro, Col., 137, 138
Mzilikazi, 18, 20, 22

Natal, 16, 18, 23–5, 26, 90, 138
Neethling, Japie, 135

Orange Free State, 36, 90, 133, 143

Paardeberg, 86, 104, 105, 107
Page, Sgt., 83
Pilcher, Col., 108
Pitsani, 37, 39, 40, 42, 43, 75
Plumer, Col., 82, 85, 86
Potgieter, Andries, 15–24
Pretorius, Andries, 24

Rebels, problem of, 106, 129, 130, 137–9, 146
Rhodes, Cecil John, 26–32, 35–45, 54, 90

Rhodesia, 26, 39, 54
Roberts, Frederick Sleigh, First Earl Roberts of Kandahar, 61, 87, 89, 90, 95, 96, 104, 108, 112, 113
Robinson, Sir Hercules, 39–40, 42
Rudd, C. D., 29
Rundle, Gen. Sir Leslie, 112, 113

Salisbury, Lord, 87, 106
Schalk Burger, President, 142, 144
Schoenmann, Mrs., 136
Scorched earth policy, 136, 143
Sheldon, Col., 140
Slavery, 10, 15
Smith, Capt., 24
Smuts, Jan Christian, 49–50, 66, 67, 116, 128, 130, 132–4, 135–43, 145–8
Snyman, Commandant, 80, 81, 86
South African Republic, 33
Stephenson, T. E., 100, 102
Steyn, President M. T., 47, 48, 50, 106, 108, 114, 115, 116, 143, 144, 145, 147, 148
Stormberg, Battle of, 57–8, 62

Tilney, Capt., 64
Transvaal, 25, 31–2, 33, 35–7, 90, 143, 144, 145, 148
Typhoid fever, 124

Uitlanders, 34, 35, 40–43, 45, 48
Union of South Africa, 148
Vendutie Drift, 92–104

Vereeniging Conference, 141, 142–7
Victoria, Queen, 74
Volksraad, 22

Walford, Col., 80
Warren, Maj. Gen. Sir Charles, 32
Wauchope, Brig. Gen. A. J., 56–7
Weil, Benjamin, 76

White, Lt. Gen. Sir George, 54, 73
Whitewash Report, 126
Wilhelm II, Kaiser, 45, 74
Wilhelmina, Queen, 140
Witwatersrand, 34

Zulu War, 62
Zulus, 16, 23
Zwaar Kop, 115

Also by James Barbary

THE CRIMEAN WAR

The Crimean War came after thirty-nine years of peace between the Great Powers. Though British troops were probably the best-drilled and smartest in the world – and when it came to the test they showed unbounded courage – the men at the top were not used to command. Administration broke down; the army was badly supplied with food and munitions, and the sick and wounded were neglected. For blunders, tactical errors and misunderstanding, the Crimean War has no equal in modern times. Of the 60,000 crack troops who left Britain in 1854, 43,000 were dead or disabled by January 1855. Only 7,000 of these had fallen in battle; cholera, exposure and starvation took care of the rest.

But the war did bring about enormous changes. It loosened the grip on the British Army of rich aristocrats who were soldiers because soldiering was fashionable. Public opinion, stirred up by the brilliant reports of William Russell in *The Times*, forced on the Government a radical improvement in the conditions under which men fought. And the inspired sacrifice and hard work of Florence Nightingale ensured that military hospitals at last became organised to *save* lives. The war also helped along one of the most far-reaching changes in history – the awakening of the Russian peasant from his long centuries of serfdom.

TO BE A SLAVE

Julius Lester

Can you imagine what it must have been like to be a slave? Can you think of yourself as being owned by somebody else, just as you might own a dog, or a bicycle or a table or chair? As a slave you had no rights of any kind. Your owner could sell you if he wished, separating you from your wife, or husband, or home, or child, completely as the whim took him.

This book tells you what it must have been like. It is constructed from the memories of ex-slaves taken from the records of the American Anti-Slavery Society and many other Northern abolition groups, recorded both before and after the American Civil War, and the excerpts are linked together by Julius Lester into a history of the Black Americans.

THE DODO, THE AUK AND THE ORYX

Robert Silverberg

'As dead as a dodo' is a sadly common expression. Sad because no one in living memory has ever seen a dodo, and the world is a sadder place for it. But how many other creatures have we driven, or are we driving, to extinction?

In the fifty years between 1851 and 1901 thirty-one kinds of mammal disappeared, and today about 600 forms of animal life are near vanishing point. Robert Silverberg tells the story of some of these birds and beasts which have vanished from the earth and others which have been rescued from extinction, or rediscovered when they were thought to have disappeared forever. Today we are making some effort to preserve our wild life: it is worth preserving. Just imagine how dull the world would be without tigers, elephants, humming-birds, aardvarks and kangaroos!

THE BOOMERANG BOOK

M. J. Hanson

Do you know how to make a boomerang bounce? Can you throw it so that it circles a tree or post and then returns to you? Can you make it fly back past you and return to you?

In this book M. J. Hanson tells you how to make and throw your own boomerangs. He gives clear step-by-step instructions for both right-handed and left-handed boomerang throwers and with a little patience and a little woodwork skill you will produce a boomerang that will make you the envy of your friends.

Join the ancient art of boomerang throwing. It's fun, it's cheap and it's catching.

THE PAPER AEROPLANE BOOK

Seymour Simon

What makes paper aeroplanes soar and plummet, loop and glide? Why do they fly at all?

This book will show you how to make them and explains why they do the things they do. Making paper aeroplanes is fun and, by following the author's step-by-step instructions and doing the simple experiments he suggests, you will also discover what makes a real aeroplane fly. As you make and fly paper planes of different designs, you will learn about lift, thrust, drag and gravity; you will see how wing size and shape and fuselage weight and balance affect the lift of a plane; how ailerons, elevators and the rudder work to make a plane dive or climb, loop or glide, roll or spin. Once you have grasped these principles of flight, you will be ready to take off with designs of your own.

EXPLORERS

A series of non-fiction titles for children between 10 and 12 years of age, Explorers are readable, informative and visually exciting. Explorers are 48 pages in extent and approximately half of these pages contain illustrations in full colour and black and white.

They are published jointly by Kestrel Books in hardback and Puffins in paperback.

JOURNEY TO THE PLANETS
Peter Ry anand Ludek Pesek

ABOUT DINOSAURS *Margery Morris*

PLANET EARTH *Peter Ryan and Ludek Pesek*

THE OCEAN WORLD
Peter Ryan and Ludek Pesek

HOW MAN BECAME *Margery Morris*

GOLD AND GRANITE *Susan Brennand*

THE DISCOVERY OF AMERICA
J. R. L. Anderson

THE DAY OF THE COWBOY *Kenneth Ulyatt*

PIRATES OF THE SPANISH MAIN *Douglas Botting*

ON BURIED AND SUNKEN TREASURE
Rupert Furneaux

THE LIVING SEA *Ritchard Read*

DIGGING INTO THE PAST *Shirley Kay*

VOLCANOES *Rupert Furneaux*

THE VIKINGS *J. R. L. Anderson*